How to Write a Children's Picture Book

Volume II: Word, Sentence, Scene, Story

How to Write a Children's Picture Book

Volume II: Word, Sentence, Scene, Story

Learning from
Leo the Late Bloomer,
Harry the Dirty Dog,
Lilly's Purple Plastic Purse,
Harold and the Purple Crayon,
and Other Favorite Stories

Eve Heidi Bine-Stock

E & E Publishing
Sausalito, California

Copyright © 2006 Eve Heidi Bine-Stock
ISBN 0-9748933-2-3

E & E Publishing,
a Registered Trade Name of
THE E & E GROUP LLC
1001 Bridgeway, No. 227
Sausalito, California 94965
U.S.A.
Website: www.EandEGroup.com/Publishing
Email: EandEGroup@EandEGroup.com

Publisher's Cataloging-In-Publication Data
(Prepared by The Donohue Group, Inc.)

Bine-Stock, Eve Heidi.
    How to write a children's picture book / Eve Heidi Bine-Stock.

    v. : ill. ; cm.

    Includes bibliographical references and indexes.
    Contents: v. 1. Structure -- v. 2. Word, sentence, scene, story --
v. 3. Figures of speech.
    ISBN-13: 978-0-9719898-8-7 (v. 1)
    ISBN-10: 0-9719898-8-5 (v. 1)
    ISBN-13: 978-0-9748933-2-7 (v. 2)
    ISBN-10: 0-9748933-2-3 (v. 2)
    ISBN-13: 978-0-9748933-4-1 (v. 3)
    ISBN-10: 0-9748933-4-X (v. 3)

1. Picture books for children--Technique. 2. Picture books for
children--Authorship. I. Title.

PN147.5 .B56
808/.06/8

Printed in U.S.A.

Dedication

For my loving husband, Edward, who believes in happy endings.

Contents

Part II

Contents

Introduction

Whereas Volume I of this series investigates the overall structure of children's picture storybooks at the macro level, this volume, Volume II, investigates the very building blocks of picture storybooks at the micro level: the word, the sentence, the scene and the story.

We look at the importance of word choice for giving the story meaning and cohesion.

We look at ways to change sentence structure to emphasize the information that is important, and to ensure that sentences flow easily from one to another.

We look at the scene: how to begin it, how to end it, and how to create the Beats of action-reaction that make up the scene.

And finally we look at the story: what types of problems must a character solve? When does a story introduce a problem? And once a problem is introduced, how do picture storybooks move from problem to solution? What types of solutions do characters find? Is there any part of a story that occurs *after* the solution is found? To answer these and other questions is to describe storytelling strategies. We look at enduringly popular children's picture storybooks to see what storytelling strategies they employ.

Part I

The Word

The word is the first building block of a story and is the first tool in the writer's toolbox. Let us look at the importance of word choice.

Harold and the Purple Crayon begins with:

> One evening, after thinking it over for some time, Harold decided to go for a walk in the moonlight.

By choosing the word *moonlight,* the author has set up the story to end easily and logically with Harold in bed, dropping off to sleep. It is the perfect bedtime story.

But what if the author had used *day* instead of *evening,* and *sunlight* instead of *moonlight?*

> One day, after thinking it over for some time, Harold decided to go for a walk in the sunlight.

This is a very different story. Now, in order to create a bedtime story that ends with Harold in bed, dropping off to sleep, the author would have had to create additional steps, such as Harold drawing the sun setting and then the moon rising. It wouldn't be the elegant story that it is.

Let us look at the importance of word choice in *Where the Wild Things Are*. One night Max is wild and gets into all sorts of mischief. The story tells us:

> ... Max said "I'LL EAT YOU UP!"
> so he was sent to bed without eating anything.

Let us look at that word *eat*. The author, Maurice Sendak, could have written:

> so he was sent to bed without his supper

but he didn't. He wrote:

> so he was sent to bed without eating anything

thereby repeating the word *eat* and creating unity between the two sentences.

Later in the story, the author repeats the same idea of being sent to bed without eating, but states it in different words:

> Max...sent the wild things off to bed without their supper.

Why didn't the author write "without eating anything" as he had done before? Because now he was setting up a smooth transition to the last scene in the book when Max returned to his room and "found his supper waiting for him and it was still hot." By repeating the same idea of being sent to bed without eating, but rewording the idea to introduce the word *supper*, Sendak creates unity between these two sentences and scenes.

With careful study we can see how Sendak creates very smooth step-by-step transitions. First, he creates a smooth transition from "I'll eat you up" to "sent to bed without eating anything" by repeating the word *eat*.

Then, he creates a smooth transition by repeating the same idea of being sent to bed without eating anything, but stating it in different words, "sent to bed without supper."

Finally, having introduced the word *supper*, he creates another transition from "Max...sent the wild things off to bed without their supper" to the last scene when Max returned to his room and "found his supper waiting for him and it was still hot." In this step-wise fashion and with the careful selection of *eat* and *supper*, Sendak creates smooth transitions.

Let us look at another example of the importance of word choice. In *Corduroy* by Don Freeman, the story begins with:

> Corduroy is a bear who once lived in the toy department of a big store. Day after day he waited with all the other animals and dolls for somebody to come along and take him home.

First of all, your grammar teacher would tell you that you should write "a bear that," not "a bear who." The word *who* is supposed to be reserved for people, and is not to be used for animals and inanimate objects. By using *who*, the author has anthropomorphized Corduroy, that is, has given him human characteristics—which is the intended effect.

Let us examine another word choice in this excerpt. Look what happens if we change "...he waited for somebody to come along and take him home" to "...he waited for somebody to come along and buy him."

What effect does this change in word choice have?

First of all, one does not buy an individual who is *real*—who has human characteristics. So this word choice—"buy him"—makes it harder for the reader to imagine that Corduroy is "real"—can think and talk and want to be loved.

Second, by using "buy him" instead of "take him home," we lose the resonance with the end of the book, when Corduroy looks around the room he will share with the little girl and says, "This must be home. I *know* I've always wanted a home!"

As you can see, you must choose your words as carefully as if you were writing a poem.

Note that in both *Harold and the Purple Crayon* and *Corduroy*, the word choice at the beginning of the story is important for setting up closure with the end. When the end echoes the beginning, it contributes to the story's cohesion, giving the reader a sense of completion and a sense of satisfaction. The concept of cohesion is so important that it has a chapter of its own.

The Sentence—Focus & Rhythm

After the word, the sentence is the next building block of a story. Sentences have a rhythm, with some words receiving more stress. This is also called intonation.

To be in control of the message that the reader gets from a sentence, you must understand sentence rhythm, and place the important information where the sentence naturally receives the most stress.

In short, simple sentences, we tend to focus on the information at the end:

Frog and Toad went for a walk.
Corduroy searched for his button.
Sylvester turned into a stone.
Harry ran away from home.

In addition to the character name, you probably stressed *walk, button, stone and home.* Children's picture storybooks are filled with this kind of sentence.

As a writer, you can intentionally shift the stress of a sentence by using various tools in the writer's toolbox[1]. This will not only help you direct the

---

[1] Inspired by chapter 2 of *Rhetorical Grammar: Grammatical Choices, Rhetorical Effects*. Third Edition. Martha Kolln. Allyn & Bacon, 1998.

reader's attention to what is important, it will also add variety and interest to the rhythm of your story. Your goal should be to use these tools *effectively*, not necessarily frequently.

Here are some of these tools:

The Comma

The common comma can be used to change the rhythm of a sentence. Let us see how this can be done by looking at an example from *Leo the Late Bloomer*.

After the narrator recites a litany of things that Leo cannot do (can't read, write, draw, and so on), the list ends with:

And, he never said a word.

That comma adds stress, length and rising intonation to the word *And*. We can almost hear the drum roll as we wait to learn what else Leo cannot do.

In fact, a comma always adds stress, length and rising intonation to the word immediately preceding it. (In the preceding sentence, you probably stressed *fact*, thanks to that comma.)

Try reading the sentence about Leo again, this time without that comma:

And he never said a word.

You stressed *never* and *word*, didn't you?

Ah, the power of a comma!

That comma in *Leo the Late Bloomer* is important, not just for the drum-roll effect, but because it clarifies the meaning of the sentence; we understand that Leo never spoke. Without that comma (*And he never said a word*), we might interpret the sentence to mean that Leo never complained about all the things he couldn't do.

Changing Word Order

You can control which part of a sentence is emphasized by changing the word order in specific ways. Here we discuss three common techniques.

The Adverb-Shift

You can shift the emphasis of a sentence to the beginning by shifting the placement of an adverb to the beginning.

For example, in Act II of *Corduroy*, during the bear's nocturnal adventure, we read:

—and up he went!

And up he crawled onto a large, thick mattress.

Off came the button....

—and off the mattress Corduroy toppled....

Over it fell with a crash!

In *Corduroy*, this technique of beginning a sentence with an adverb—thereby shifting the stress to the beginning—is used only in Act II and nowhere else. What is happening in Act II that requires a special technique? Corduroy is searching for his button, exploring unknown territory, and getting into all kinds of mischief. We see that he is inquisitive, adventurous, spunky and, yes, *lively*. A special technique—the adverb shift—creates a special sentence rhythm that emphasizes Corduroy's special character.

The *It*-Shift

By starting a sentence with "It is," "It was," "It has been," and so on, you shift the emphasis to the part of the sentence immediately following the "It...."
Look at these examples:

It was a terribly frightening dragon.
> *- Harold and the Purple Crayon*

It was a great day for a picnic.
> *- The Stray Dog*

You probably emphasized *terribly* and *great*, didn't you?

The *There*-Shift

Here we begin a sentence with "There is," "There was," "There are," and so on, in order to shift the emphasis to the part immediately following the "There...."

Look at these examples from the *Harold and the Purple Crayon*:

There was nothing but pies.
But there were all nine kinds of pie that Harold liked best.

You stressed *nothing* and *all nine kinds*, didn't you?

Power Words

Some words just naturally command attention, and when you use them, they shift the focus and rhythm of a sentence. (That word *naturally* is one of them!) Let us look at some examples from popular children's picture storybooks:

That very night in Max's room a forest grew...
            - Where the Wild Things Are

He jumped into the bathtub and sat up begging, with the scrubbing brush in his mouth,

a trick he certainly had never done before.
                    - Harry the Dirty Dog

They even took trips downtown.
                    - Lyle, Lyle, Crocodile

Leo is just a late bloomer.
                    - Leo the Late Bloomer

In the above examples, you probably stressed *very, certainly, even* and *just.* Try reading these sentences again, leaving out the key words. What a difference you'll see!

Time, Frequency, Duration

Words that express time, frequency and duration tend to be stressed. Consider these examples:

Day after day he waited with all the other animals and dolls for somebody to come along and take him home.
                    - Corduroy

Lyle could spend hours watching building construction.
                    - Lyle, Lyle, Crocodile

And they always refused to do their lessons.
                    - Miss Nelson is Missing!

He still couldn't find the king.
> *- Harold and the Purple Crayon*

In these examples, you probably stressed *day after day*, *hours*, *always* and *still*.

Superlatives

Superlatives are adjectives that express the extreme degree of comparison such as *best* and *brightest*. Have a look at these examples:

They were the worst-behaved class in the whole school.
> *- Miss Nelson is Missing!*

Harry's bath was the soapiest one he'd ever had.
> *- Harry the Dirty Dog*

...the smallest one was Madeline.
> *- Madeline*

In these examples, you probably stressed *worst*, *soapiest* and *smallest*.

Closely related to the superlatives are words loaded with emotional power:

On a rainy Saturday during vacation he found a quite extraordinary one.
> *- Sylvester and the Magic Pebble*

"What a fantastic pebble!" he exclaimed.
> *- Sylvester and the Magic Pebble*

Lyle wanted desperately to win Loretta over.
> *- Lyle, Lyle, Crocodile*

Did you stress *extraordinary, fantastic* and *desperately*?

Not only/but also

The pair *Not only/but also* belongs to a category of power words that grammar teachers call "correlative conjunctions." Other, similar pairs of power words include *either/or, neither/nor, both/and, not only/but...as well*.

These pairs shift the emphasis and rhythm of a sentence. They are not very common in children's picture storybooks, but they do have their place. For example, in "A Lost Button" from *Frog and Toad Are Friends* by Arnold Lobel, Toad says,

Not only do my feet hurt, but I have lost one of the buttons on my jacket.

How different that sentence sounds from the alternative:

My feet hurt and I have lost one of the buttons on my jacket.

The alternative sounds flat in comparison. The original has more "punch."

Sentence, Sentence, Sentence— Cohesion

When sentences are connected to one another, when the text flows, and when the separate sentences of a story become a unified whole, the story is said to have *cohesion*.

Cohesion is important because it helps your story meet the reader's expectations and gives the reader a sense of satisfaction.

We shall look at specific tools in the writer's toolbox that you can use to give your story cohesion[2].

Parallelism

Parallelism is the repetition of words, phrases or rhythms which have a similar structure. Parallelism can be created within a single sentence, and between sentences and scenes. Using parallelism increases the cohesion of a story.

Here are some examples of parallelism within a single sentence:

Being helpless, he felt hopeless.
            - Sylvester and the Magic Pebble

[2] Inspired by chapter 3 of *Rhetorical Grammar: Grammatical Choices, Rhetorical Effects*. Third Edition. Martha Kolln. Allyn & Bacon, 1998.

Night followed day and day followed night over and over again.
　　　　- Sylvester and the Magic Pebble

In fact, he changed from a white dog with black spots to a black dog with white spots.
　　　　- Harry the Dirty Dog

He flip-flopped and he flop-flipped.
　　　　- Harry the Dirty Dog

Now let us look at some examples of parallelism *between* sentences and scenes.

Here are sentences that Corduroy speaks which echo each other:

"I think I've always wanted to climb a mountain."

"I guess I've always wanted to live in a palace."

"I've always wanted to sleep in a bed."

"I *know* I've always wanted a home!"

"I've always wanted a friend."

In *Millions of Cats*, the following lines are repeated and become a refrain:

Hundreds of cats,
Thousands of cats,
Millions and billions and trillions of cats.

A common use of parallelism is to show progression. Just look at these sentences taken from succeeding pages of stories:

...got very dirty.
...got even dirtier.
...became dirtier still.
...got the dirtiest of all.
                              - Harry the Dirty Dog

But that didn't seem likely.
But that didn't seem likely either.
But that was the least likely of all.
                              - Miss Nelson is Missing!

Here is an exercise for you: study *Leo the Late Bloomer* and determine all the ways that it exhibits parallelism. You will discover that it is a masterpiece!

Known-New Pattern

Readers have expectations when they read a story. They read the first sentence and then expect the second sentence to relate to what came before. They also expect that second sentence to provide new information. And they expect subsequent sentences to follow this same pattern.

These expectations are so strong that those who study Rhetoric call this the Known-New pattern.

Probably the simplest example of the Known-New pattern is the use of pronouns.

Let us look at the story "A Lost Button" from *Frog and Toad Are Friends*. The first sentence is, "Toad and Frog went for a long walk." The next sentence is, "They walked across a large meadow."

The pronoun *They* in the second sentence refers to *Toad and Frog* in the first sentence. This, together with *walk/walked*, constitutes the known information that ties the two sentences together before the new information, "across a meadow," is introduced.

In this way, we employ the Known-New pattern without even thinking about it.

A more sophisticated example of the Known-New pattern can be seen in *Corduroy*. The first page of the story tells us that Corduroy is a bear. The second page repeats the word *bear* (the known information), and adds new information, "...a small bear in green overalls."

Harold and the Purple Crayon is an excellent example of the use of the Known-New pattern. In fact, this story actually emphasizes the Known-New pattern.

The first page of the book has only one sentence, and it ends with "go for a walk in the moonlight."

The second page continues with the idea of *walk* and *moonlight* (the known information) and extends it by introducing new information, "There wasn't any moon and Harold needed a moon for a walk in the moonlight."

The third page continues with the known *walk* information, and adds new information, "And he needed something to walk on."

And so on. As we progress through the story, we cannot wait to see what the new information will be—what the new twist will be. The continuous use of the Known-New pattern is one of the main reasons we find the book so charming.

Another example of a story that relies on the Known-New pattern is *If You Give a Mouse a Cookie*. Can you think of others?

Sentence Focus

Take a look at the following two sentences:

A) Mommy Mouse gave Little Mouse a gift.
B) Mommy Mouse gave a gift to Little Mouse.

They mean the same thing, but the focus is different. In the first sentence, the focus is on the gift, while in the second sentence, the focus is on Little Mouse.

If these were two versions of the first sentence of a story, what would you expect the follow-up sentence to look like in each case?

Here are three possibilities:

1. It was a pair of mittens that she had knitted herself.
2. She had gone to every shop in town looking for the perfect hat.
3. He asked, "Is today my birthday?"

Can you match the most likely follow-up sentence with A and B above?

Your own knowledge of the language tells you that the reader expects the follow-up sentence to pick up with the focus of the previous sentence.

Let us look at another example, this one from *Corduroy* by Don Freeman. The story begins with:

Corduroy is a bear who once lived in the toy department of a big store. Day after day he waited with all the other animals and dolls for somebody to come along and take him home.

The emphasis here is that Corduroy waits for *somebody to take him home*. The very next sentence of the story follows up on this idea:

The store was always filled with shoppers buying all sorts of things, but no one ever seemed to want a small bear in green overalls.

Now, what happens if we make a small change in the structure of one of the sentences at the beginning of the story? An alternate version of the beginning might be:

Corduroy is a bear who once lived in the toy department of a big store. Waiting day after day for somebody to come along and take him home, he stood with all the other animals and dolls.

Here the emphasis is on Corduroy standing *with all the other animals and dolls.* This leads us to believe that the story is about Corduroy and the other animals and dolls. We might expect the next sentence to be something like:

At night, when the store was quiet, Corduroy led them up and down the escalators.

You can see from these examples that the structure of a sentence is critical in setting up the reader's expectations about what is important, and what will come next. If "what comes next" relates to what the reader thinks is important, the story will have cohesion.

Sentence Order

Children's picture books often begin with two sentences that set up the story. The order of the sentences is important. Just as the reader expects the end of a single sentence to get the emphasis, the reader expects the second sentence in a pair to get the emphasis.

In "The Letter" from *Frog and Toad Are Friends* by Arnold Lobel, Frog says:

"What is the matter, Toad? You are looking sad."

By putting the "sad" part at the end of the second sentence, the author has emphasized it.

Note that Frog does **not** say:

"You are looking sad, Toad. What is the matter?"

This alternate version emphasizes the *problem* that is making Toad sad, while Mr. Lobel's version emphasizes Toad's *sadness*.

Mr. Lobel's version also sets up our expectation that the sentence which follows will relate in some way to Toad's sadness—which it does:

"What is the matter, Toad? You are looking sad."

"Yes," said Toad. "This is my sad time of day. It is the time when I wait for the mail to come. It always makes me very unhappy."

If the author had written the alternate version instead—

"You are looking sad, Toad. What is the matter?"

—the reader would expect the sentence which follows to relate to "what is the matter." In this case, the sequence might look something like this:

"You are looking sad, Toad. What is the matter?"

"I never get any mail."

This alternate version may be short and to the point, but we miss the whole mention of waiting which is so important to the story, and which, in fact, sets up the "punch line" or "pay-off" at the end, when Frog and Toad wait for four days until the snail delivers Frog's letter.

Let us look at an example of a scene deeper into a story than the first two sentences. Do the same principles apply?

Take *Leo the Late Bloomer* by Robert Kraus and look at Plot Twist I[3], the scene where Leo's mother and father are discussing what is wrong with Leo. Leo's mother assures his father that there is nothing wrong; Leo is just a late bloomer. The scene ends with Leo's father saying, "Better late than never."

Now, what do you expect the next sentence to begin with? Leo's father, or Leo? Let's take a look:

Every day Leo's father watched him for signs of blooming.

So we see that the next sentence picks up with Leo's father. This sentence is the first sentence of Act II, and all of Act II focuses on Leo's father watching—and then not watching—Leo for signs of blooming. And how was that set up? By giving Leo's father the last word at the end of one scene, and following up with Leo's father in the next.

You can probably already guess how the book makes the transition from Act II, with Leo's father watching and not watching, to Plot Twist II when Leo blooms, but let's take a look anyway. Pay close attention to sentence order. The end of Act II is:

The trees budded.
Leo's father wasn't watching.
But Leo still wasn't blooming.

---

3 For a discussion of the structure of *Leo the Late Bloomer*, see pgs. 79-84, *How to Write a Children's Picture Book Volume I: Structure.* Eve Heidi Bine-Stock, E & E Publishing, 2004.

Plot Twist II now begins with the very next sentence. Can you guess who will be the subject? Leo's father, or Leo? If you guessed Leo, you are right:

Then one day, in his own good time,
Leo bloomed!

By ending Act II with Leo, and starting Plot Twist II with Leo, the writer met the reader's expectations about what would come next, and thereby created a smooth transition.

You can see from these examples that sentence order is critical in setting up the reader's expectations about what is important, and what will come next. If "what comes next" meets the reader's expectations, the story will have cohesion.

Sentence after Sentence—
Action & Reaction

We have looked at the reader's expectations for a single sentence, and we have looked at the reader's expectations as he moves from one sentence to another.

What other information do we need to know in order to write sentence-after-sentence to craft a scene? *We need to know that the reader expects every action to have a reaction.* Successful picture storybook authors know this, whether intuitively or consciously.

There are two types of action: inner and outer. An outer action is something a character *does* or *says*. An inner action is something a character *thinks, feels, senses* or *wants*.

Actions prompt reactions, and there are two types of reaction, inner and outer, just like actions.

Let us look at some examples:

...Toad went into the house and stood on his head [outer actions]. "Why are you standing on your head?" asked Frog [outer reaction].
- "The Story" from *Frog and
Toad Are Friends*

...Toad gave his jacket to Frog [outer action]. Frog thought that it was beautiful [inner reaction]. He put it on and jumped for joy [outer reactions].

> - "A Lost Button" from *Frog and Toad Are Friends*

A character can also react to his *own* action:

> Toad baked some cookies [outer action]. "These cookies smell very good," said Toad [outer reaction]. He ate one [outer action]. "And they taste even better," he said [outer reaction].
>
> - "Cookies" from *Frog and Toad Together*

A *condition* (rather than an action) can also prompt a reaction. For example:

> When Harold finished his picnic, there was quite a lot [of pie] left [condition]. He hated to see [inner reaction] so much delicious pie go to waste. So Harold left [outer reaction] a very hungry moose and a deserving porcupine to finish it up.
>
> - *Harold and the Purple Crayon*

In addition to an action and a condition, a *thing* (called an agent) can prompt a reaction:

The sandy beach [thing/agent] reminded Harold [inner reaction] of picnics.

- Harold and the Purple Crayon

Order: Action-Reaction and Not Reaction-Action

The author of a children's picture storybook knows that the reader expects the reaction to *follow* the action, not come *before* the action.

Here is an example of the faulty reaction-action pattern[4]:

Willy caught the ball after Joey tossed it.

There is nothing wrong with that sentence grammatically, but you can see that writing the opposite order—reaction first, then action—creates a momentary hesitation for the reader and impedes easy comprehension.

Let us look at that interaction again, this time in the proper order, action-reaction:

Joey tossed the ball. Willy caught it.

All of the examples in this chapter follow the action-reaction pattern. Because this pattern is so

---

4 This example inspired by an example on page 21 of *Scene & Structure*. Jack M. Bickham. Writer's Digest Books, 1993.

much easier to understand, children's picture story-books rely on it.

Inner Versus Outer

Let us review two examples in order to study the kind of reactions authors write about—inner versus outer.

> ...Toad gave his jacket to Frog [outer action]. Frog thought that it was beautiful [inner reaction]. He put it on and jumped for joy [outer reactions].
>
> > - "A Lost Button" from *Frog and Toad Are Friends*

> When Harold finished his picnic, there was quite a lot [of pie] left [condition]. He hated to see [inner reaction] so much delicious pie go to waste. So Harold left [outer reaction] a very hungry moose and a deserving porcupine to finish it up.
>
> > - *Harold and the Purple Crayon*

In these two examples, the story tells us not only how the characters *feel* (their inner reaction), but what they *do* (their outer reaction) as well. This is a very important point to remember. Children's picture storybooks not only tell us about the character's *inner* reaction, but also about the *outer* reaction.

To put this another way, a story does not have to tell us about the character's inner reaction, but if it does, it will not stop there. It will always follow up by telling us what the character's outer reaction is too.

Even individual sentences can be written to express an outer action. With this in mind, how could you improve the following two sentences?

Corduroy was sad as they walked away.

This was Toad's sad time of day.

Let us see what the original authors did:

Corduroy watched sadly as they walked away.

The author used the outer reaction *watched sadly*—something we would have seen if we had been there with Corduroy.

Toad said, "This is my sad time of day."

The author used the outer reaction of speaking, "Toad said...."—something we could hear if we had been there with Toad.

As you can see, the author of a children's picture storybook remembers to tell us what we would see or hear if we were actually watching the scene play out in front of us.

Of the six kinds of action and reaction—do, say, think, feel, sense, want—which ones are used most frequently in children's picture storybooks? The outer kinds, *do* and *say*, but mostly *do*—the easiest to visualize and the easiest to illustrate. It is well to keep this in mind as you write your own stories.

In addition to considering the needs and expectations of the illustrator and the reader, another important reason to employ *do* and *say* actions is that the characters in the story can react to such actions. Characters cannot react to what someone thinks, feels, senses or wants, but they can see what someone *does* and hear what someone *says*.

In *Corduroy*, the little girl tells her mother that "There's the very bear I've always wanted." Corduroy, the bear, overhears this. Of course, the writer could easily have chosen to use narration to convey the same information and tell us what the girl felt or wanted: "There was the very bear that the little girl had always wanted." But if the narration provides this information, it would not be something that Corduroy would be able to hear. And it is important to the story that Corduroy hear this.

Similarly, the mother tells the little girl that "He's lost the button to one of his shoulder straps." The writer could easily use narration convey the same information and tell us what the mother was thinking, but again, Corduroy would not be able to overhear it.

If narration *had* been used to tell us what the mother was thinking, then in order to justify Corduroy's adventures in Act II, the story would have to be changed to enable Corduroy to find out about his missing button another way, perhaps by having Corduroy notice it on his own. But then the writer would have to come up with something that would prompt Corduroy to even look down at his overalls in the first place.

We can see, then, that the best solution—for writer and character alike—is for the writer to convey all of this information through dialogue—what the characters **say**.

And by employing dialogue, the writer gives readers the sense that they are there in the department store, overhearing the customers the same way Corduroy does. And this helps us to identify with Corduroy even more.

We have said that a story does not have to tell us about the character's inner reaction, but if it does, it will follow up by telling us what the character's outer reaction is too. Let us look at a scene from "Spring" from *Frog and Toad Are Friends* where the author has omitted the character's inner reaction to good effect.

In the Second Half of Act II, Frog gets an idea for a new strategy to use in his efforts to get Toad to come outside with him. Now he will play by Toad's rules and get the better of him. When Frog sees that the calendar is still stuck on November, he tears off the pages month-by-month until he has reached May, the month for waking up Toad.

Let us look at that again: the Objective Narrator tells us what Frog sees—the November page still on the calendar (a condition)—and then the next thing we see is Frog tearing off the November page.

The Objective Narrator does not tell us what happened between these two moments. But we infer what happened: Frog *realized* what he should do next. This "coming to a realization" is a hidden, implied inner reaction, *thinking*, that is not mentioned at all in the story. Instead, the story shows us the outer reaction: Frog tears off the November page and then every page until May.

We, the readers, come to the same realization that Frog does, at the same time Frog does or a little later, as he tears off the pages. And because the author omitted mention of this inner reaction from the text, we, the readers, take pleasure in coming to this realization by ourselves.

Adding Point of View

Sometimes a reaction just does not make sense or it lacks impact unless we know what the character is reacting to. This requires the author to include the character's point of view—what he sees or hears—before he reacts. Here are some examples to see how this is done:

Frog walked into the house [outer action]. It was dark. All the shutters were closed [point of view]. "Toad, where are you?" called Frog [reaction].

> - "Spring" from *Frog and Toad Are Friends*

Up, up he sailed, higher and higher [outer action]. The houses looked like toy houses and the people like dolls [POV]. George was frightened [inner reaction]. He held on very tight [outer reaction].

> - *Curious George*

So he put a frightening dragon under the tree to guard the apples [outer action]. It was a terribly frightening dragon [POV]. It even frightened Harold [inner reaction]. Harold backed away [outer reaction].

> - *Harold and the Purple Crayon*

As you can see, the point of view (POV) is given after the action and before the reaction.

Exceptions that Prove the Rule

Let us see how breaking a rule actually proves that the rule exists in the first place.

For Every Action There is a Reaction

Authors know that the reader expects the rule "for every action there is a reaction" to be followed. The skilled author can intentionally break this rule in order to achieve a particular effect.

For example, the intentional *lack* of a reaction can be used to create suspense or mystery:

> Frog ran up the path to Toad's house and knocked on the door [outer actions]. There was no answer [lack of reaction].
> - "Spring" from *Frog and Toad Are Friends*

We are left wondering, where is Toad?

The Wolf's Chicken Stew is another example of the author intentionally omitting reaction.

Each time the wolf leaves food on the chicken's porch—with the goal of fattening her up for his stew—the author withholds from the reader the chicken's reaction.

It is not until the end that we discover—together with the wolf—that it was the hen's houseful of baby chicks that ate all the food, thereby foiling the wolf's plan.

Had the author written the chicken's reaction to the food on the porch each time, there would have been no surprise and much of the enjoyment of the story would have been lost.

In the story *Corduroy*, the main character *doesn't* react to the key action of the story, but why isn't the reader disappointed? Let's see.

When we read *Corduroy* and we get to the part where the little girl goes back to the store and tells Corduroy that she is going to take him home, why doesn't Corduroy react right then and there? After all, we saw him walking and talking earlier when he tried to find his button. Why does he only react once he gets to the little girl's room? And why don't we notice a "hole" in the story where Corduroy's reaction is supposed to be? Questions, questions, questions!

Corduroy may be "real," but he is real only to children; he does not speak when he is in the presence of grown-ups. Remember how he kept silent when the night watchman spoke to him? (The author cleverly had the night watchman ask a rhetorical question— "How did *you* get upstairs?—to which the night watchman did not expect a reply, and neither did we.)

Similarly, when the little girl returns to the store and tells Corduroy that she is going to take him home, Corduroy does not react because this interaction takes place in the presence of the saleslady. But why don't we notice a "hole" in the story where Corduroy's reaction was supposed to be? Because the author had the saleslady speak, instead: "Shall I put him in a box for you?"

Now that that pesky "hole" has been filled, the little girl's answer to this question provides an opportunity to affirm Corduroy's status as "real": she says "no thank you" and carries Corduroy home in her arms, the same way one carries a baby. After all, you wouldn't carry a baby or a friend or anyone with human characteristics, in a box!

You can see that a careful analysis of the story provides answers, answers, answers.

Reaction Follows Action Promptly

Authors know that the reader expects the reaction to follow the action promptly. You have seen this to be the case in the examples already given.

This rule can also be broken by the skilled author in order to achieve a particular effect.

In "The Letter" from *Frog and Toad Are Friends*, Frog gives a letter to a snail and asks him [actions] to take it to Toad's house and put it in his mailbox. The snail says, "Sure. Right Away" [reaction].

The author takes advantage of the reader's expectation that the continued reaction will follow promptly, in order to set up a joke. The snail delivers the letter "right away" [reaction], but his "right away"—because he is a snail—is four days later!

No Reaction Without a Preceding Action

You have seen in all of the examples in this chapter that there is no reaction without a preceding action, condition or agent that prompts the reaction.

This is certainly the rule but exceptions can be found where the action, condition or agent is intentionally omitted.

Let us look at an example from "Spring" from *Frog and Toad Are Friends*. Frog acts by pushing Toad out of bed, out of the house and onto the porch. Toad then reacts by blinking and saying "Help! I cannot see anything!"

What is interesting here is that Toad's reaction is not in response to Frog's action. If it were, Toad might say something like, "Stop pushing me!" But he doesn't; he blinks and complains that he cannot see.

What is Toad actually reacting to? It is the action of sunlight striking him, or the condition of lightness/brightness outside, in contrast to the darkness inside his home, to which he was accustomed.

Why don't we notice that an action or condition is missing here? And why aren't we confused by Toad's reaction? Because the author had previously taken care to tell us Toad's house was dark inside. So when Frog pushes Toad outside, the author does not have to slow the story down to remind us that it is light outside in contrast to the darkness inside.

By omitting this action or condition here, and maintaining the rapid pace of the scene, the author heightens the dramatic impact of Toad's reaction.

Action Sequence

We have said that for every action there is a re-action, but this is not strictly true: there is also something called an action sequence which is a sequence of actions (say, five to nine actions) uninterrupted by an intervening reaction.

Unless the action sequence occurs at the Mid-point or Mid-Spot, action sequences tend to come in pairs so that one action sequence is "balanced" by the other.

Let us look at some examples.

In *Leo the Late Bloomer*, Act I has an action sequence of five things that Leo cannot do (read, write, draw, eat, speak), and then Act III has a complementary action sequence of five things that Leo *can* do (read, write, draw, eat, speak).

In "Spring" from *Frog and Toad Are Friends*, there is an action sequence (in the First Half of Act II) of nine *say* actions of Frog telling Toad what they can do together in spring:

1. Don't be silly
2. You see the light of April
3. We can begin a new year together
4. Think of it
5. Skip through meadows
6. Run through woods
7. Swim in river
8. Sit on porch
9. Count stars

and a complementary, balancing action sequence (in the Second Half of Act II) of nine *do* actions of Toad tearing off pages of the calendar.

1. Frog looked at calendar
2. November page on top
3. Frog tore off November page
4. Tore off December page
5. and the January page
6. the February page
7. the March page
8. He came to the April page
9. Frog tore off April page, too

Let us look at the pair of action sequences in *Yoko*. In Act I, there is an action sequence of seven *do* actions of children eating different kinds of food for lunch:

1. Timothy unwrapped a peanut butter and honey sandwich.
2. Valerie had cream cheese and jelly.
3. Fritz had a meatball grinder.
4. Tulip had Swiss cheese on rye.
5. Hazel had egg salad on pumpernickel.
6. Doris had squeeze cheese on white,
7. and the Franks had franks and beans.

And later, in the First Half of Act II, there is a corresponding action sequence of nine *do* actions of the children bringing different food for International Day:

1. Valerie and her mother carried in a plate of enchiladas.
2. Timothy and his mother made Caribbean coconut crisps.
3. Hazel brought Nigerian nut soup.
4. Harry brought Brazil nuts.
5. Doris brought Irish stew.
6. Tulip brought potato knishes.
7. Monica brought a pitcher of mango smoothies.
8. Fritz brought spaghetti.
9. Big Frank cooked up a pot of Boston franks and beans.

These three examples show the importance of balancing one action sequence with a complementary one later in the story.

The Beat—Building Block of a Scene

We have seen how to write sentence-after-sentence to create an action-reaction unit. Screenwriters refer to such a unit as a *Beat*. This term is also helpful to us as children's book writers.

Robert McKee tells us[5]:

---

[5] See pages 37-38 of *Story: Substance, Structure, Style and the Principles of Screenwriting*. Robert McKee. HarperCollins, 1997.

"A Beat is an exchange of behavior in action/reaction. Beat by Beat these changing behaviors shape the turning of a scene."

Let us look at "Spring" from *Frog and Toad Are Friends* for an example of how Beats may be joined together to build a scene. To paraphrase McKee, let us take the single Story Event, the "Toad refuses to wake up" scene. This scene is built around six Beats, six distinctively different behaviors, six clear changes of action-reaction:

1. Frog trying from outside to wake up Toad
2. Frog entering Toad's house and finding Toad in bed
3. Frog pushing Toad out of bed and onto the front porch
4. Frog trying to convince Toad of the beauties of April
5. Toad going back to bed
6. Toad reasoning with Frog and telling him to wake him at "half past May"

Before sitting down to write sentence-after-sentence of an action-reaction unit, it is a good idea to list the Beats in the order they will appear in your scene. Then you can concentrate on writing the action-reaction sequence that makes up a single Beat, and then progress from Beat to Beat until you have completed the scene.

Summary

To review, here are "rules" that we have learned about in this chapter:

1. Every action has a reaction.
2. Reactions do not just happen; an action occurs first.
3. Sentences show action first, reaction after.
4. Reactions follow actions promptly.
5. Outer reactions are given, not just inner reactions.
6. When point of view is given, it comes after the action and before the reaction.
7. An early action sequence is balanced by a later action sequence

Go over your own stories and see if you have followed these "rules," unless you have intentionally broken them to create a special effect.

The Link

Scenes are made up of Beats of action-reaction that propel the story forward toward a goal. In addition to the overriding goal of the story as a whole, each scene has its own mini-goal. Once the scene goal is achieved (or not), how is a new goal set for the next scene? This is very often done through a story unit which I call the *Link*.

In the Link, the viewpoint character reacts to what has just happened to him, then sets his next (short-term) goal, and plans the course of action he will take to achieve that goal.

Consider *Harry the Dirty Dog*. Harry's first goal is to avoid getting a bath. After he hides the scrubbing brush and runs away from home, his goal is to have fun playing. After he has played for quite some time, we encounter the first Link in the story:

> Although there were many other things to do, Harry began to wonder if his family thought that he had <u>really</u> run away. He felt tired and hungry too, so without stopping on the way he ran back home.

In this Link, Harry first looks back at his preceding actions and thinks about the consequences. He assesses how he feels now, sets a new goal (to return home) and takes action to achieve his new goal (he runs home without stopping).

As you can see, in this Link, Harry looks back, then looks ahead; this segment is thus a link between what came before and what comes next.

Later in the story, after Harry returns home, he sits in the backyard looking at the back door. One of the family looks out and sees a strange dog and asks, "has anyone seen Harry?" At this point, a Link appears in the story:

> When Harry heard this, he tried very hard to show them <u>he</u> was Harry. He started to do his old, clever tricks.

In this Link, Harry considers what has just happened to him (his family doesn't recognize him), and sets a new goal (to convince them that <u>he</u> is Harry). He decides what action he will take (do his old, clever tricks) to achieve his new goal.

As in the previous Link, in this Link, Harry looks back, then looks ahead; this segment is a link between what came before and what comes next.

In spite of Harry's tricks, his family says, "Oh, no, it couldn't be Harry." Now another Link appears:

> Harry gave up and walked slowly toward the gate, but suddenly he stopped. He ran to a corner of the garden and started to dig furiously.

In this Link, Harry reacts to what has just happened to him (gives up and walks slowly toward the gate), then sets a new goal (to get the scrubbing brush so he can have a bath), and takes action to achieve his goal (he runs to a corner of the garden...).

In this Link, as in the others, Harry looks back, then looks ahead to a new goal; this segment is a link between what came before and what comes next.

Is *Harry the Dirty Dog* the only children's picture storybook that has Links? Not at all. Let us take a look at some others.

In *Yoko*, the Link that jumps out at us is the scene in which Yoko's teacher, Mrs. Jenkins, frets about what has happened to Yoko that day in class, sets a new goal (to have Yoko's food choice accepted by her classmates), then decides what action to take to solve the problem: she writes a letter to the parents, inviting them to International Food Day at school.

This Link in *Yoko* follows the same pattern as the Links in *Harry the Dirty Dog*: the character looks back, then looks ahead; reacts to what has happened, sets a new goal, and decides how to achieve it.

In *The Wolf's Chicken Stew*, after Mrs. Chicken has foiled the wolf's plan by introducing him as "Uncle Wolf" to her chicks and fixing him a nice dinner, we find this Link:

"Aw, shucks," he thought, as he walked home, "maybe tomorrow I'll bake the little critters a hundred scrumptious cookies!"

This Link follows the same pattern we have seen before: the character looks back, then looks ahead; reacts to what has just happened ("Aw, shucks"), sets a new goal (to be a good uncle and please the chicks), and decides what to do next to achieve that goal (bake cookies). The segment is a link between what came before and what comes next.

In *Corduroy*, a particularly pivotal scene is, in fact, a Link. After Corduroy overhears the exchange between the little girl and her mother, we have this Link:

"I didn't know I'd lost a button," he said to himself. "Tonight I'll go and see if I can find it."

Remember the pattern of the Link? The character looks back, then looks ahead; reacts to what has just happened, sets a new goal, and decides how to achieve it. This Link in *Corduroy* follows the pattern.

In *Fish is Fish*, after the frog has regaled the fish with stories of the strange creatures he has seen on land, we have the following relatively long Link:

And so the days went by. The frog had gone and the fish just lay there dreaming about birds in flight, grazing cows, and those strange animals, all dressed up, that his friend called people.

One day he finally decided that come what may, he too must see them. And so with a mighty whack of the tail he jumped clear out of the water onto the bank.

This Link follows the same pattern we have learned: the character looks back, then looks ahead; reacts to what has just happened, sets a new goal, and decides how to achieve it.

Lilly's Purple Plastic Purse has two extended Links; we shall discuss one here.

Shortly after Lilly has sneaked a mean drawing into her teacher's book bag, she discovers in her purse a nice note and tasty snacks that he has placed inside. Next we find a Link in the story in which Lilly reacts to this discovery. First, she reacts emotionally:

Lilly's stomach lurched.
She felt like crying.
She felt simply awful.

Then Lilly punishes herself by sitting in the uncooperative chair. Next, she sets a new goal (to apologize to her teacher) and decides what action to take to remedy the situation: she draws a new picture of her teacher and writes a story about him. The next day, armed with her new picture and story, and her mother's note and her father's tasty snacks, she offers her gifts and apologies to her teacher.

This Link follows the same pattern as the other Links we have seen: Lilly looks back, then looks ahead; she reacts to what has just happened, then sets a new goal (to apologize to her teacher) and decides how to achieve her goal.

We said earlier that this story has two extended Links. Can you find the other one by yourself?

We can see from the above examples that the goal does not have to be expressed. It may be implied from the action taken. The goal need only be explicitly stated if it is needed for the reader to understand the purpose of the action that is taken next.

We can also see that the Link may be as short as one sentence and as long as several pages. The key to the Link is the pattern: the character looks back, then looks ahead; reacts to what has just happened, then sets a new goal and decides what course of action he will take to achieve that goal.

The Link tends to be longer if the emotional impact is stronger and the character need not act immediately. The Link in *Lilly's Purple Plastic Purse* is a good example of this. Lilly reels from her discovery of her teacher's note and tasty snacks in her purse and is deeply mortified. The Link shows us every aspect of her reaction in great detail. Furthermore, Lilly does not have to face her teacher immediately; she has all evening to react, to set a new goal, and to prepare to achieve her goal.

A Weak Link

Until now we have examined well-written Links. But Links are not necessarily easy to write. The well-loved *Caps for Sale* provides a surprising example of an ill-written Link.

The peddler has just spent a morning peddling caps without success. "Nobody wanted even one red cap." Now we read the following Link:

> He began to feel very hungry,
> but he had no money for lunch.
> "I think I'll go for a walk in the country,"
> said he.

We now expect the peddler to look in the country for food—berries or apples or some such. But does he do this? No! He looks for a place to rest instead.

A much better Link would have been something like the following:

> He began to feel very tired,
> but he could not find a nice place to rest.
> "I think I'll look for some shade in the country,"
> said he.

This Link would have correctly set up our expectation for what comes next, his finding a tree to rest under.

And this is the key: a Link sets up our expectations for what comes next; what follows the Link must flow from the Link—it cannot be a different subject entirely.

Omitting a Link

A Link has the effect of slowing the pace of a story. For this reason, there are times when you, the author, would choose *not* to write a Link.

A good example of a "missing" Link is in *The Stray Dog*. When the boy and girl catch up to the dog warden who has caught Willy, the dog warden says, "He has no collar. He has no leash. This dog is a stray. He doesn't belong to anybody." What happens next?

> The boy took off his belt.
> "Here's his collar," he said.
> The girl took off her hair ribbon.
> "Here's his leash," she said.
> "His name is Willy and he belongs to us."

Notice that the boy and girl acted *immediately*, They didn't have the luxury of time to feel, think or plan—and so the author dispensed with a Link altogether.

Signaling the Beginning
of a Scene

No special fanfare or signal is needed to begin the very first scene of a story; we can enter the action *without* any introductory phrase such as, Once upon a time....

Subsequent scenes, however, may need a signal to set the scene off from the preceding one, to indicate that we are about to start something *new*. This is especially true when the new scene occurs at a new time or place.

For example, *Sylvester and the Magic Pebble* is a story that consistently signals the beginning of a new scene by referring to a new time or place:

On a rainy Saturday during vacation...

As he was crossing Strawberry Hill...

Meanwhile...

After a month...

Night followed day...

Then it was winter.

Then the snows melted.

One day in May...

When they had eventually calmed down...

Bread and Jam for Frances is another example of a story that consistently signals the beginning of a new scene by referring to a new time or place:

While she waited for the bus...

That evening for dinner...

The next morning at breakfast...

When the bell rang for lunch...

Then she went out to the playground...

When Frances got home...

The next day when the bell rang for lunch...

In addition to signaling the beginning of a new scene by referring to a new time or place, the writer may need to indicate a change in *action*. This is most often done by using "signal" words and phrases such as *suddenly, all of a sudden, just then, all at once.*

In *Corduroy*, after the bear climbs down from his shelf and begins searching on the floor for his lost button, a new scene starts with a signal word that indicates new action:

Suddenly, he felt the floor moving under him!

Later, after Corduroy has crawled onto a mattress, a new scene starts—or at least a shift in focus occurs when the story moves from one shot to another shot within the current scene. A signal phrase is used to indicate new action in the new scene/shot:

All at once he saw something small and round.

The signals we have been discussing provide a smooth transition from one scene to the next. Their consistent—even repetitive—use within a story also contributes to that story's rhythm and cohesion.

In spite of this, most of the stories we examine usually signal the *end* of a scene, and do not employ a special signal to indicate the *beginning*.

One way to think of the difference between these two approaches is the difference in music between accenting the *last* beat of a four-beat measure, and accenting the *first*.

As we shall see in the next chapter, signaling the beginning of a scene is relatively simple compared to the many techniques available for signaling the end.

Signaling the End of a Scene

As readers, we sense when we have come to the end of a scene. What specific tools or techniques does the writer use to signal to readers that the end of a scene has arrived? To answer this question, we shall study the techniques used by enduringly popular children's picture storybooks.

Reaction

One of the most common ways to end a scene is with a reaction. For example, in *Miss Nelson is Missing!*, the scene showing the ways in which the kids misbehave ends with Miss Nelson's reaction:

> "Something will have to be done," said Miss Nelson.

In *Harry the Dirty Dog*, the scene in which Harry does tricks in an attempt to convince his family that he is really Harry, ends with the family's reaction:

> ...but everyone shook his head and said, "Oh, no, it couldn't be Harry."

In *Sylvester and the Magic Pebble*, the scene with the lion ends with the lion's reaction:

"I saw that little donkey as clear as day. Maybe I'm going crazy," he muttered.

In *Corduroy*, the scene in which the bear tells the little girl that he's always wanted a friend ends with the little girl's reaction:

"Me too!" said Lisa, and gave him a big hug.

Ending a scene with a reaction is a technique that *Lilly's Purple Plastic Purse* uses frequently. In fact, this story employs such reactions as a refrain. The scene describing Mr. Slinger ends with:

"Wow," said Lilly.... "Wow."

The scene in which Lilly is at home, pretending to be Mr. Slinger, ends with:

"Wow," said her father.... "Wow."

The scene describing Lilly's creativity during Lightbulb Lab and Sharing Time ends with:

"Wow," said Mr. Slinger.... "Wow."

The scene in which Lilly apologizes to Mr. Slinger ends with:

"Wow," said Mr. Slinger.... "Wow."

The scene in which Lilly demonstrates her purse, quarters and sunglasses, and then dances, ends with:

"Wow," said the entire class.... "Wow."

As you can see, these similar reactions at the end of these scenes create a refrain.

Corduroy is another story that creates a refrain by using similar reactions to end scenes and shots within scenes. The shot in which Corduroy goes up an escalator ends with:

"Could this be a mountain?" he wondered. "I think I've always wanted to climb a mountain."

The first shot of the furniture department scene, in which Corduroy first finds himself in this amazing place, ends with:

"This must be a palace!" Corduroy gasped. "I guess I've always wanted to live in a palace."

The second shot of the furniture department scene, in which Corduroy first sees a bed, ends with:

"This must be a bed," he said. "I've always wanted to sleep in a bed." And he crawled onto a large, thick mattress.

The first shot of the scene in the little girl's room ends with:

"This must be home," he said. "I *know* I've always wanted a home!"

As you can see, these similar reactions at the end of these shots create a refrain.

"Signal" Words

Another common way to signal the end of a scene is with "signal" words such as *And, So, But, And then, And soon* and *Even.*

After Mr. Slinger takes Lilly's purse away, the scene ends with the signal word *even*:

She was even too sad to eat the snack Mr. Slinger served before recess.

In *Leo the Late Bloomer*, the sequence showing all the things Leo cannot do ends with the signal word *And*:

And, he never said a word.

In *Harry the Dirty Dog*, the scene in which Harry steals and hides the scrubbing brush ends with the signal word *then*:

Then he ran away from home.

Power Words

Power words are words that we naturally emphasize. (We discussed power words in an earlier chapter.) A scene might end with such an emphatic word, as in the scene from *Lilly's Purple Plastic Purse* in which Lilly discovers Mr. Slinger's nice note and bag of snacks at the bottom of her purse:

She felt simply awful.

Here, *awful* is naturally emphasized, and since it appears at the very end of the sentence—and the scene—it provides a sense of finality.

In *Where the Wild Things Are*, the opening scene in which Max is wild ends with the power word *anything*:

...so he was sent to bed without eating anything.

In *Miss Nelson is Missing!*, after the kids realize that Miss Nelson is not coming to class—and before Miss Swamp appears—the scene ends with a combination of the power words *just terrible*, and an exclamation point:

"Today let's be just terrible!" they said.

In *Tikki Tikki Tembo*, when Chang is rescued from the well and resuscitated, the scene ends with a combination of the power word *ever* and an exclamation point:

"...and soon Chang was just as good as ever!"

Superlatives

We naturally emphasize superlatives and this emphasis helps give a sense of finality to a scene. (We discussed superlatives in an earlier chapter.)

In *Miss Nelson is Missing!*, the scene in which the kids speculate about what happened to Miss Nelson ends with a superlative:

But that was least likely of all.

In *Where the Wild Things Are*, the scene in which Max tames the wild things ends with a superlative:

...and they were frightened and called him the most wild thing of all and made him their king.

Another scene later in this same story ends with a superlative:

And Max...wanted to be where someone loved him best of all.

"Signal" words, combined with superlatives, are also often used to end a scene. Examples are *And most of all* and *And best of all*.

The scene from *Lilly's Purple Plastic Purse* that describes everything Lilly loves about school ends with a sentence containing a signal word and a superlative:

And, most of all, she loved her teacher, Mr. Slinger.

The scene from this same story that tells us what Lilly bought on her shopping trip ends with a sentence containing a signal word and a superlative:

And, best of all, she had a brand new purple plastic purse that played a jaunty tune when it was opened.

Reference to a Future Time

Another way to signal the end of a scene is by referring to a future time when something will happen.

For example, in the scene from *Yoko* in which Yoko's teacher, Mrs. Jenkins, is trying to reassure

Yoko, the scene ends with a reference to a future event:

> "They'll forget about it by snack time," said Mrs. Jenkins.

In another scene from *Yoko*, Yoko's mother is trying to reassure Yoko that the upcoming International Food Day will be a success for Yoko. The scene ends with a reference to the future event:

> "Don't worry, my little cherry blossom, everyone will try our sushi and everyone will love it!

In a scene from *Lilly's Purple Plastic Purse*, Lilly's parents are trying to reassure Lilly about what will happen when she apologizes to her teacher, Mr. Slinger, the next day. The scene ends with references to that future time:

> "I think Mr. Slinger will understand," said Lilly's mother.

> "I know he will," said Lilly's father.

In *Sylvester and the Magic Pebble*, the scene in which Sylvester discovers the magic powers of his pebble ends with a reference to actions that will happen in a future time:

He could hardly wait to see their faces. Maybe they wouldn't even believe him at first.

Later in the same book, the scene in which Sylvester's parents are worried because he is late for dinner ends with his mother's promise to do something in a future time:

"I will never scold Sylvester again as long as I live," said Mrs. Duncan, "no matter what he does."

In *Corduroy*, the scene in which the bear learns that he is missing a button ends with a reference to actions that will happen in a future time:

"Tonight I'll go and see if I can find it."

A variation of this idea of a reference to a future time is ending a scene before an anticipated action happens. For example, in *Miss Nelson is Missing!* the kids see Miss Swamp coming around the corner near Miss Nelson's house.

"If she sees us, she'll give us more homework."
They got away just in time.

Summary or Conclusion

Some scenes signal the end with a summary or conclusion based on the preceding action.

The scene from *Leo the Late Bloomer* in which Leo's mother explains what is wrong with Leo, ends with a conclusion by Leo's father:

"Better late than never," thought Leo's father.

The last scene in the book ends with a conclusion by Leo, himself:

"I made it!"

In *Sylvester and the Magic Pebble*, the scene in which his parents try to adjust to his permanent absence, ends with a very sad conclusion:

Life had no meaning for them any more.

In *Miss Nelson is Missing!*, the first scene with Detective McSmogg ends with a humorous conclusion:

Detective McSmogg would not be much help.

In Harry the Dirty Dog, the sequence of Harry getting dirty ends with the summary or conclusion:

In fact, he changed from a white dog with black spots, to a black dog with white spots.

Later in this same book, the scene of Harry digging up the scrubbing brush and begging to be bathed ends with a summary or conclusion:

...and he became once again a white dog with black spots.

The end of "The Letter" from *Frog and Toad Are Friends* ends with a conclusion:

Four days later the snail got to Toad's house and gave him the letter from Frog. Toad was very pleased to have it.

The end of *Yoko* ends with a conclusion:

And they couldn't have asked for anything more.

Had

Another way to signal the end of a scene is with a "summarizing" phrase that uses the word *had*.

For example, in *Yoko*, at the end of International Day, the scene ends with *had*:

But no one had touched even one piece of Yoko's sushi.

In *Lilly's Purple Plastic Purse*, when the children file out of the classroom, the scene ends with *had*:

....Mr. Slinger was right, it *had* been a better day.

In *Sylvester and the Magic Pebble*, when Sylvester's parents ask the neighbors and children if they have seen him, the scene ends with *had*:

No one had seen Sylvester since the day before.

The very last scene of *Sylvester and the Magic Pebble* ends with another *had*:

They all had all that they wanted.

The last scene of "A Lost Button" from *Frog and Toad Are Friends* ends with *had*:

None of the buttons fell off.
Toad had sewed them on very well.

In *Harry the Dirty Dog*, the last scene of the book ends with a form of *had*:

He slept so soundly, he didn't even feel the scrubbing brush he'd hidden under his pillow.

Remember, *he'd* is a contraction of *he had*.

The End of a (Natural) Period of Time

By ending a scene at the end of a natural period of time, such as the end of the day, or the end of the week, season or year, the reader intuitively understands that this is the end of the scene.

For example, in *Sylvester and the Magic Pebble*, the scene in which Sylvester is first turned into a rock ends with the end of the day:

Night came with many stars.

In *Corduroy*, the night watchman sets Corduroy on the shelf in the toy department alongside the sleeping animals and dolls, and the picture shows us that Corduroy has fallen asleep too. It is the end of the day and the end of the scene.

In *The Stray Dog*, the scene of the family thinking about Willy during the work week, Monday through Friday, actually ends at the end of the work week, on Friday. This is another example of the end of a "natural" period of time.

Warning

A writer might signal the end of a scene with a warning, as in this example from *Tikki Tikki Tembo*:

"Don't go near the well," warned the mother, "or you will surely fall in."

In *Leo the Late Bloomer*, the scene in which Leo's father watches him day and night for signs of blooming, ends with a warning by Leo's mother:

"A watched bloomer doesn't bloom."

Another example of a warning (together with a reaction) ending a scene is from *Strega Nona*:

"The one thing you must never do," said Strega Nona, "is touch the pasta pot. It is very valuable and I don't let anyone touch it!"

"Oh, *si*, yes," said Big Anthony.

Ellipsis

The definition of ellipsis that I use here is a scene or action that can be thought of as continuing indefinitely into the (untold) future, as though there were an ellipsis ("...") at the end of the sentence.

This technique is not often used within the body of the story. As we shall see, it is more commonly used at the end of the very last scene of a book.

However, one example of an ellipsis that *can* be found within the body of a story is in *Sylvester and the Magic Pebble*. Sylvester has turned into a rock and much time has passed. It is now winter. The winter scene ends with the following ellipsis:

> One day a wolf sat on the rock that was Sylvester and howled and howled because he was hungry.

As you can see, we are given the impression of the howling continuing indefinitely into the future.

Another example of an ellipsis that occurs within the body of the story is in *Make Way for Ducklings*. Mr. and Mrs. Mallard are looking for a place to live. Every time Mr. Mallard sees what looks like a nice place, Mrs. Mallard says that it is no good.

> So they flew on and on.

In this example, we are given the impression of the flying continuing indefinitely into the future.

Signaling the End of a Story

The previous chapter dealt with techniques for signaling the end of a scene. Many of the same techniques for ending a scene are employed for ending a story since, after all, the end of a story is the end of the last scene of the book.

However, there are some techniques that are more or less unique to signaling the end of a story. I refer to these techniques as Bedtime, Ellipsis and Echo.

Bedtime

Perhaps because children's picture storybooks are so often read to children before they go to sleep, stories often end at the end of the day when the characters go to sleep.

"The Surprise" from *Frog and Toad All Year* ends with:

> That night Frog and Toad were both happy when they each turned out the light and went to bed.

Similarly, "The List" *from Frog and Toad Together* ends with:

Then Frog and Toad went right to sleep.

Harold and the Purple Crayon ends similarly with:

The purple crayon dropped on the floor,
And Harold dropped off to sleep.

The Stray Dog ends with Willy curled up asleep on his bed, along with the following text:

And Willy settled in where he belonged.

Make Way for Ducklings ends with:

And when night falls they swim to their little island and go to sleep.

Ellipsis

The definition of ellipsis that I use here is a scene or action that can be thought of as continuing indefinitely into the (untold) future, as though there were an ellipsis ("...") at the end of the sentence. A particularly familiar ellipsis is, "And they lived happily ever after."

A good example of an ellipsis appears at the end of "Spring" from *Frog and Toad Are Friends*:

Then he and Frog ran outside to see how the world was looking in the spring.

Another example of an ellipsis appears at the end of "Dragons and Giants" from *Frog and Toad Together*:

They stayed there for a long time, just feeling very brave together.

"The Letter" from *Frog and Toad Are Friends* ends with a similar ellipsis:

They sat there, feeling happy together.

Martha Speaks ends with the following ellipsis:

Now Martha eats a bowl of alphabet soup every day. She's learning what to say and when to say it, and sometimes she doesn't say anything at all...at least for a few minutes.

Echo

Many picture storybooks end with an echo, which I define as the repetition of a central idea introduced at or near the beginning of the book.

For example, *Harry the Dirty Dog* begins with Harry stealing the scrubbing brush from the tub, and ends with the following echo:

He slept so soundly, he didn't even feel the scrubbing brush he'd hidden under his pillow.

Corduroy begins with the bear waiting for someone to take him home, and ends with the following echo:

"You must be a friend," said Corduroy.
"I've always wanted a friend."

Me, too!" said Lisa, and gave him a big hug.

Come Along, Daisy begins with Mama Duck telling Daisy to "stay close" and ends with the following echo:

And even though Daisy played with the butterflies...she stayed very close to Mama Duck.

Caps for Sale uses a combination of an ellipsis and an echo at the end of the story when it repeats the peddler's call we heard near the beginning of the story:

And slowly, slowly, he walked back to town calling, "Caps! Caps for sale! Fifty cents a cap!"

As you can see, the echo technique contributes cohesion to the story and gives the reader a sense of closure and thus a sense of satisfaction.

The Art of Selection

So much of our understanding and enjoyment of a story revolves around the art of selection—the author's decisions about what to put in and what to leave out. For example, does the author state the character's goal, or have us figure it out for ourselves? Even the absence or appearance of a single word can entirely change the meaning of a passage. Let us look at some examples where the art of selection affects the reader's experience.

In *The Wolf's Chicken Stew*, the wolf gets a craving for chicken stew and finally spots a chicken walking in the forest. The author writes:

> But just as he was about to grab his prey...
> [turn page]
> he had another idea.
> "If there were just some way to fatten this bird a little more," he thought, "there would be all the more stew for me." So...
> [turn page]
> the wolf ran home to his kitchen, and he began to cook.

In the above passage, the author tells us the wolf's goal, but does not tell us how the wolf decides to achieve that goal; we just jump right to the wolf cooking in his kitchen.

It would be redundant if the author had the wolf say to himself, "I'll cook food for the chicken to fatten her up," and then the next scene shows him cooking in the kitchen. It would not only be redundant, it would ruin the surprise and humor that we experience when we turn the page and see the wolf cooking in his kitchen. This is a good example of writing as the art of selection, deciding what to put in and what to leave out.

At the end of the story, the wolf abandons his original goal of fattening up the chicken and establishes the new goal of being a good uncle and pleasing the little chicks.

> "Aw, shucks," he thought, as he walked home, "maybe tomorrow I'll bake the little critters a hundred scrumptious cookies!"

Here the wolf has made a new, tentative, decision about what action he will take, and the author lets us know what the decision is. When we turn the page, we see that the wolf has followed through, not because we see him cooking in the kitchen, but because the picture shows the chicks eating a basketful of cookies. This is another example of writing as the art of selection.

Let us look at another example of the art of selection from *Harry the Dirty Dog*:

Harry gave up and walked slowly toward the gate, but suddenly he stopped. He ran to a corner of the garden and started to dig furiously.

In this passage, Harry decides to dig up scrubbing brush, but the author does not tell us, "Harry decided to dig up the scrubbing brush." We see only Harry's action: he ran to the corner of the garden and started to dig furiously. From this we *infer* that his goal is to dig up the scrubbing brush.

By leaving out the *decision* of what action to take, and just showing us the action, the author not only keeps up the pace, he keeps us actively engaged in the story by having us *think* about what Harry's goal is, and we take pleasure in figuring out what Harry is up to.

We take a similar pleasure in "Spring" from *Frog and Toad Are Friends* when Frog sees that the calendar is stuck on November and the author only shows us Frog's action of tearing off subsequent months of the calendar. The author never states Frog's goal (to fool Toad into thinking months have passed), and we take pleasure in figuring out for ourselves what Frog doing. This is another example of the art of selection—of the author deciding what to put in and what to leave out.

The art of selection can also revolve around a single word. For example, in *Sylvester and the Magic Pebble*, Sylvester holds the magic pebble and says, "I wish it would stop raining." Let's read what happens next:

To his great surprise the rain stopped. It didn't stop gradually as rains usually do. It CEASED. The drops vanished on the way down, the clouds disappeared, everything was dry, and the sun was shining as if rain had never existed.

In the above excerpt, the first time the author mentions rain, he writes *the rain*. The last time he mentions rain, he writes simply *rain* ("the sun was shining as if rain had never existed"). By omitting the single word *the* here, the author conveys the idea that even the *concept* of rain, not just a particular instance of rain, had never existed. All of that by the simple art of selection.

Number of Characters & Number of Plots

It is almost a rule: each character in a children's picture storybook has his own plot or subplot that is given closure. Very often these plots or subplots continue to the end of the story.

If a writer introduces a character and then leaves him and his plot dangling, the reader will likely wonder what happened to him and feel dissatisfied that the character and his plot were not given closure. It is important to continue the characters and their plots through to the end of their storyline—which is often to the very end of the story—in order to give the reader a sense of satisfaction.

In children's picture storybooks, when characters are not mentioned again in the text at the end, they are made to appear in the illustrations.

Let us look at some examples.

Leo the Late Bloomer has three characters and each character has his own plot. The main plot revolves around Leo, of course, and his inability to do anything right. There is a subplot revolving around Leo's father and his impatience with the time it takes Leo to bloom. Another subplot revolves around Leo's mother and her role as the oracle of the family who voices words of wisdom.

Even though Father and Mother are not mentioned again in the text after Leo blooms, they appear in the pictures at the end in order to continue and tie up their subplots.

Lyle, Lyle, Crocodile has the following characters introduced in the text:

Lyle
Mr. Grumps' cat, Loretta
Mr. Grumps
Joshua
Mrs. Primm
Signor Hector P. Valenti

Each character has his own plot or subplot that weaves its way through the story and all of these characters appear at the end; only Joshua is not mentioned at the end but he appears there in the illustrations.

In *Where the Wild Things Are*, there is one main character, Max, and one supporting character, his mother. Even though we never actually *see* Max's mother, we hear her near the beginning of the story, and see the result of her actions at the end of the story since we understand that it was she who left Max's supper for him.

In *Yoko*, the storyline involving her mother is given closure on the back cover of the book, where Yoko and her mother are smiling over a sushi tray—literally a happy ending.

As we can see from these examples, it is important for both the writer and illustrator to remember that each character has his own plot or subplot that weaves its way through the story and should be given closure, which often means being tied up at the very end.

Story Dynamics

Every story has direction and movement of forces—dynamics. It is important that you understand the direction and movement of the story you are writing, and that you do not interrupt its flow.

Let us look at *Harry the Dirty Dog* to understand this better.

Harry runs away from home to avoid taking a bath. He then plays in the dirt so much that he changes from a white dog with black spots to a black dog with white spots. Wondering if his family thinks he has *really* run away, and being tired and hungry too, he returns home.

At this point, the author writes:

When Harry got to his house,
he crawled through the fence
and sat looking at the back door.

Now, Harry is a very active dog, so the question is: why didn't Harry go up to the back door and scratch at it to be let in? Why did he stay in the back yard and sit looking at the back door, "willing" the family to look at him?

If he *had* scratched at the back door, the close proximity of Harry to the family at the back door would require the family to interact directly with Harry. There would likely be one of two reactions:

1. A confrontation: "Who are you? You're not Harry. Go away! Shoo!"
2. An invitation: "Well, hello there! Who are you? Are you hungry? Let me get you something to eat."

The invitation clearly turns the story in the wrong direction as far as the writer is concerned, while the confrontation makes the family appear too mean.

The distance—Harry in the back yard and not at the back door—absolves the family of having to interact directly with Harry.

Instead, the author writes:

One of the family looked out and said,
"There's a strange dog in the back yard...
by the way, has anyone seen Harry?"

But there is another reason that Harry does not go up to the back door: that action would be counter to the direction and movement of forces—the dynamics—of the story.

The story as the author wrote it has the following flow: Harry runs from inside the home out to the big, wide world. Then he goes from the big, wide world into the home. We can call this the "back and forth" dynamic.

If Harry *had* gone up to the back door, then in order for him to perform his tricks, he would have had to *turn around and go back* to the back yard. He would have had to go in a direction *counter* to the flow of the story.

The author, however, understood the direction and movement of forces—the dynamics—of his story, and did not bring Harry up to the house prematurely.

Another story that employs the "back and forth" dynamic is *Where the Wild Things Are*.

Other stories have other dynamics. *Leo the Late Bloomer* and *Sylvester and the Magic Pebble* both employ the cycle—the circle—of the seasons, and let the story come full circle before the resolution takes place.

Corduroy, "Spring" from *Frog and Toad Are Friends*, and *Good Night, Gorilla* all employ a "tug-of-war" dynamic in which the opposing characters end up on the same side at the end of the story.

Bread and Jam for Frances, Come Along, Daisy and *Martha Speaks* employ the "spike" dynamic: a sharp rise of exaggerated, unacceptable behavior followed by a sharp drop to conformity with the baseline of acceptable behavior.

There are other dynamic patterns, to be sure. The important point to remember is that your characters should act in accordance with the dynamic of the story they find themselves in.

Part II

Story—Problem & Solution

The meat and potatoes of picture storybooks are problems and solutions.

What types of problems do we find in picture storybooks? When does a story introduce a problem? At the very beginning? Sometime later? If the story does not start with a problem, what does it start with and when does it introduce a problem? And once a problem is introduced, how do picture storybooks move from problem to solution? What types of solutions are there? Is there any part of a story that occurs *after* the solution has been found? In short, what storytelling strategies are used? We shall look at enduringly popular children's picture storybooks to see how they answer these questions.

We must first decide which kind of storybook structure to consider. Traditional story structure builds to a single, major climax, followed by a resolution. Episodic story structure has a series of episodes, each one having its own buildup, climax and resolution. We shall look at the more common traditional story structure.

If you have read the first volume of *How to Write a Children's Picture Book*, you will recall that traditional story structure most often follows the Symmetrical Paradigm. Therefore, we shall consider symmetrical stories and study the storytelling strategies that they employ.

We shall also consider examples of stories that follow the less-common Iterative Paradigm. We shall discover that they employ the same storytelling strategies that symmetrical stories do.

This examination of storytelling strategies does not claim to be exhaustive. It does not account for *all* storytelling strategies that you will encounter, but it does deal with the most common ones.

Kinds of Problems

There are two kinds of problems in picture storybooks that the main character most commonly has. One is the kind that can be solved by someone doing something that meets the main character's needs. This is the "needs satisfaction" story.

Examples of the "needs satisfaction" story are *Corduroy, Miss Nelson is Missing!, Leo the Late Bloomer*, "The Letter" from *Frog and Toad Are Friends, Stone Soup, Owen, Yoko, Sylvester and the Magic Pebble*, and *Millions of Cats*.

The inverse of the "needs satisfaction" story is the "needs frustration" story in which the need is *not* met such as in *The Wolf's Chicken Stew*.

The second kind of problem in picture storybooks that the main character commonly has can only be solved by a change in the character himself. He must come to a realization, make a decision, or have a change of heart, usually in order to overcome a character flaw. This is the "character transformation" story.

Examples of the "character transformation" story are *Harry the Dirty Dog*, *Come Along Daisy*, *Where the Wild Things Are* and *Bread and Jam for Frances*.

The inverse of the "character transformation" story is the "character validation" story in which the character's trait is (usually) fine the way it is and does not change despite others' efforts. Such a story is *The Story of Ferdinand*.

We shall be looking at these stories in detail.

Introducing the Problem

Some stories plunge us immediately into the midst of a problem at the very beginning of the story, without showing us what life was like beforehand. These stories employ Problem First storytelling strategies. An example of a Problem First story is *Leo the Late Bloomer*.

Other stories start out with everything going well for the characters, when suddenly a problem arises. These stories employ Background First storytelling strategies. An example of a Background First story is *Owen*.

Still other stories begin with a character's interesting behavior and "string us along" for a while before we find out the reason for the behavior. These are Action First stories. An example of an Action First story is *A Chair for My Mother*.

As we shall see, the nature of the problem, as well as when the problem is introduced, influence how the story will unfold.

Number of Problems

Most picture storybooks that follow the Symmetrical or Iterative Paradigm have only one problem that the character must solve. However, some stories have more than one problem. In these cases, the number of problems to solve is usually *two*—no more than that.

Examples of stories with two problems to be solved are *Corduroy*, *Lilly's Purple Plastic Purse*, *The Selfish Giant*, *Martha Speaks*, *Tikki Tikki Tembo*, and *A Chair for My Mother*.

We shall look at these in detail and see that they elaborate on the basic storytelling strategies used in one-problem stories.

Problem First Storytelling Strategies

We have said that the nature of the problem, as well as when the problem is introduced, influence how the story will unfold, that is, the storytelling strategy that is used.

"Needs Satisfaction" Stories – P D A W S O and P D A I S O Strategies

If a "needs satisfaction" story introduces the problem at the very beginning of Act I, the rest of Act I shows or develops the problem. Then, at Plot Twist I[6], a character sets out to solve the problem and meet the need. Act II shows things getting progressively worse (rarely progressively better). At Plot Twist II, the problem is solved, the need met. Act III shows life after the problem is solved.

A "shorthand" for this storytelling strategy might be: P D A W S O (Problem, Development, Action, Worse, Solution, Outcome), which could be pronounced "pee-dawso."

As we shall see, examples of stories that employ the P D A W S O storytelling strategy are *Miss Nelson*

---

[6] See the Appendix for definitions of Plot Twist I & II.

is Missing!, *Leo the Late Bloomer*, "The Letter" from *Frog and Toad Are Friends* and *Millions of Cats*.

An uncommon variant of the P D A W S O storytelling strategy is the P D A I S O strategy (Problem, Development, Action, *Improved*[7], Solution, Outcome), where in Act II things get progressively better rather than worse. P D A I S O could be pronounced "pee-dayso."

Stone Soup is an example of a story that employs the P D A I S O storytelling strategy.

"Needs Frustration" Story – P D A I F O Strategy

The "needs frustration" story is similar to the "needs satisfaction" story but differs in that Act II shows things getting progressively better rather than worse, and at Plot Twist II, the need is *not* met.

A "shorthand" for this storytelling strategy might be: P D A I F O (Problem, Development, Action, Improved, Frustrated, Outcome), which could be pronounced with a long "a" to sound like "pee-dayfo."

The Wolf's Chicken Stew is an example of a story that employs the P D A I F O storytelling strategy.

---

[7] The word *Improved* is used here instead of *Better* because the letter "B" is reserved for the word *Background*, as we shall see later, in the section on Background First storytelling strategies.

This section gives examples of stories that employ the Problem First storytelling strategy. We shall see that the problem type is more commonly "needs satisfaction" than "needs frustration."

Miss Nelson is Missing!

- **A "Needs Satisfaction" Story**
- **Problem First**
- **P D A W S O**

The structure of *Miss Nelson is Missing!* is symmetrical[8], the problem type is "needs satisfaction," and the storytelling strategy is P D A W S O (Problem, Development, Action, Worse, Solution, Outcome).

Act I: [P]: Introduces problem at the very beginning: Kids misbehave in class. The teacher, Miss Nelson, needs the kids to behave for her.

The Rest of Act I: [D]: Development: Shows or elaborates the problem: The many ways the kids misbehave: they whisper, giggle, squirm, make faces, fly paper airplanes, refuse to do lessons....

Plot Twist I: [A]: A character sets out to solve the problem: Miss Swamp comes to class to teach.

Act II: [W]: Things get progressively worse: Kids suffer under the rule and ruler of Miss Swamp. They search for, but cannot find, Miss Nelson. Not even the Police Detective can find her.

Plot Twist II: [S]: The problem is solved, the need met: Miss Nelson returns. The kids are happy to see her and now behave in class for her.

---

[8] The structure of this story is diagrammed in *How to Write a Children's Picture Book Volume I: Structure*. Eve Heidi Bine-Stock, E & E Publishing, 2004.

Act III: [O]: Life after the problem is solved: We learn that Miss Swamp is really Miss Nelson in disguise. In a coda, the Police Detective now searches for the now-missing Miss Swamp.

Leo the Late Bloomer
- **A "Needs Satisfaction" Story**
- **Problem First**
- **P D A W S O**

The structure of *Leo the Late Bloomer* is symmetrical[9], the problem type is "needs satisfaction," and the storytelling strategy is P D A W S O (Problem, Development, Action, Worse, Solution, Outcome).

Act I: [P]: Introduces problem at the very beginning: Leo can't do anything right.

The Rest of Act I: [D]: Development: Shows or elaborates the problem: Leo can't read, write, draw or eat neatly.

Plot Twist I: [A]: A character sets out to solve the problem: Leo's mother doesn't set out to solve the problem but she does *define* it for Leo's father: Leo is just a late bloomer. She implies that the only action to take is to wait patiently.

Act II: [W]: Things get progressively worse: Leo doesn't bloom, whether his father is watching him or not.

Plot Twist II: [S]: The problem is solved, the need met: With the passage of enough time, Leo blooms.

Act III: [O]: Life after the problem is solved: Leo can do everything right.

---

[9] The structure of this story is diagrammed in *How to Write a Children's Picture Book Volume I: Structure.* Eve Heidi Bine-Stock, E & E Publishing, 2004.

"The Letter" from Frog and Toad Are Friends

- A "Needs Satisfaction" Story
- **Problem First**
- **P D A W S O**

The structure of "The Letter" is symmetrical[10], the problem type is "needs satisfaction," and the storytelling strategy is P D A W S O (Problem, Development, Action, Worse, Solution, Outcome).

Act I: [P]: Introduces problem at the very beginning: Toad is sad.

The Rest of Act I: [D]: Development: Shows or elaborates the problem: Toad explains that he never receives a letter from anyone so waiting for the mail is a sad time for him.

Plot Twist I: [A]: A character sets out to solve the problem: Frog rushes home to write Toad a letter. Frog gives it to Snail to deliver.

Act II: [W]: Things get progressively worse: Frog tries to get Toad to continue waiting for a letter to arrive. Toad doesn't want to. Now *Frog* starts waiting.

Plot Twist II: [S]: The problem is solved, the need met: Frog admits that he sent Toad a letter. Frog

---

[10] The structure of this story is diagrammed in *How to Write a Children's Picture Book Volume I: Structure*. Eve Heidi Bine-Stock, E & E Publishing, 2004.

tells Toad what he wrote and Toad agrees that it makes a very good letter. Toad is now happy.

Act III: [O]: Life after the problem is solved: Frog and Toad wait for the letter, "feeling happy together," and when Snail finally delivers it—four days later— Toad "is very pleased to have it."

Millions of Cats

- **A "Needs Satisfaction" Story**
- **Problem First**
- **P D A W S O**

The structure of *Millions of Cats* is not symmetrical; it is iterative[11]. Nevertheless, *Millions of Cats* uses a variant of the P D A W S O storytelling strategy used by the previous four symmetrical stories. Remember, P D A W S O stands for Problem, Development, Action, Worse, Solution, Outcome. The problem type is "needs satisfaction."

Act I: [P]: Introduces problem at the very beginning: A very old couple is lonely. The very old woman wants a cat to keep them company.

The Rest of Act I: [D]: Development: Shows or elaborates the problem: Act I of this iterative story is so short that there is no room for elaboration.

Plot Twist I: [A]: A character sets out to solve the problem: The very old man sees a hill covered with cats and sets out to choose the prettiest one.

Act II: [W]: Things get progressively worse: The very old man can't decide which cat is the prettiest, so he takes them *all* home. There are so many, they wreak havoc along the way.

---

[11] See the Appendix for a definition of the Iterative Paradigm. The structure of this story is diagrammed in *How to Write a Children's Picture Book Volume I: Structure*. Eve Heidi Bine-Stock, E & E Publishing, 2004.

Plot Twist II: [S]: The problem is solved, the need met: The cats fight about which one is the prettiest. After the fight, there is only one thin, scraggly kitten left. Now the very old couple doesn't have to choose.

Act III: [O]: Life after the problem is solved: The very old couple cares for the kitten and she grows nice and plump and becomes the "most beautiful cat in the whole world."

Stone Soup

- **A "Needs Satisfaction" Story**
- **Problem First**
- **P D A I S O**

The structure of *Stone Soup* is symmetrical[12], the problem type is "needs satisfaction," and the storytelling strategy is P D A I S O (Problem, Development, Action, Improved, Solution, Outcome).

Stone Soup is unusual in that it shows things getting progressively *better* in Act II rather than progressively worse.

Act I: [P]: Introduces problem at the very beginning: Three hungry, tired soldiers need food to eat and a place to sleep.

The Rest of Act I: [D]: Development: Shows or elaborates the problem: Selfish villagers hide their food.

Plot Twist I: [A]: A character sets out to solve the problem: Soldiers announce that they will make stone soup.

Act II: [I]: Things get progressively better: Soldiers set up pots and stones for cooking. Villagers respond to the soldiers' suggestions by fetching their own hidden food for the soup.

---

[12] The structure of this story is diagrammed in *How to Write a Children's Picture Book Volume I: Structure*. Eve Heidi Bine-Stock, E & E Publishing, 2004.

Plot Twist II: [S]: The problem is solved, the need met: Villagers take the initiative to bring extravagant food for a true banquet.

Act III: [O]: Life after the problem is solved: Villagers fete the soldiers with food, wine, dancing, song—and the best beds in the village. The soldiers are treated like royalty and are given a royal send-off.

The Wolf's Chicken Stew

- **A "Needs Frustration" Story**
- **Problem First**
- **P D A I F O**

The structure of *The Wolf's Chicken Stew* is symmetrical, the problem type is "needs frustration," and the storytelling strategy is P D A I F O (Problem, Development, Action, Improved, Frustrated, Outcome).

This "needs frustration" story is the inverse of the preceding "needs satisfaction" stories. In the "needs satisfaction" stories, things get progressively *worse* during Act II and then at Plot Twist II the need is met. But in this "needs frustration" story, things get progressively *better* during Act II and then at Plot Twist II the need is *not* met.

Act I: [P]: Introduces problem at the very beginning: The wolf loves to eat.

The Rest of Act I: [D]: Development: Shows or elaborates the problem: The wolf wants to make chicken stew from the chicken that passes by.

Plot Twist I: [A]: A character sets out to solve the problem: The wolf plans to fatten up the chicken for the stew so that there is more for him to eat.

Act II: [I]: Things get progressively better: The wolf makes all kinds of food for the chicken to eat and leaves it on her doorstep.

Plot Twist II: [F]: The problem is not solved, the need is *not* met: The chicken foils the wolf's plans by exclaiming to her chicks how wonderful the wolf is for leaving all that food on their doorstep.

Act III: [O]: Life after the problem is not solved: The wolf sheepishly plans to bake cookies for the chicks as a gesture of goodwill.

Character Trait First Storytelling Strategies

This section gives examples of stories that employ Character Trait First storytelling strategies.

We shall see that the character trait is more likely to be a flaw which requires a "character transformation" to solve a problematic behavior or situation.

We shall also look at the less common type of story in which the character trait is positive, and therefore validated, in the story.

"Character Transformation" Story – C D A I W P T O Storytelling Strategy

If a "character transformation" story introduces a character flaw at the very beginning of a story, the rest of Act I shows problematic behavior stemming from that character flaw. At Plot Twist I, an action is taken by the main character or someone else that pulls the main character in the direction of his character flaw. In Act II, the character first enjoys and then suffers the consequences of his character flaw. Things get so bad that his character flaw has created a problem—a "needs satisfaction" problem. At Plot Twist II, the character comes to a realization, makes a decision, or has a change of heart that transforms his character and solves his problem. Act III shows life after his newfound maturity.

A "shorthand" for this storytelling strategy might be: C D A I W P T O (Character Trait, Development, Action, Improved/Worse, Problem, Transformation, Outcome), which could be pronounced with a long "a" and sound like "see-day-wopto."

Some stories that employ the C D A I W P T O storytelling strategy are *Harry the Dirty Dog, Come Along, Daisy, Where the Wild Things Are* and *Bread and Jam for Frances*.

"Character Validation" Story – C D A W P V O Strategy

The "character validation" story is the inverse of the "character transformation" story.

If a "character validation" story introduces a positive character trait at the very beginning of a story, the rest of Act I shows laudable behavior stemming from that positive character trait. At Plot Twist I, something happens that pulls the main character in the direction opposite to his character trait. In Act II, the character suffers the consequences of being pulled away from his natural character trait. At the end of Act II, a "needs satisfaction" problem arises—for other characters in the story. At Plot Twist II, the main character exhibits his original character trait and is validated. Act III shows life after the character trait has been validated, including other characters giving up their demand that the main character change his positive character trait.

A "shorthand" for this storytelling strategy might be: C D A W P V O (Character Trait, Development, Action, Worse, Problem, Validation, Outcome), which could be pronounced "see-daw-povo."

The Story of Ferdinand is an example of a story that employs the C D A W P V O storytelling strategy.

Let us look at some stories to see how all of this works.

Harry the Dirty Dog

- **A "Character Transformation" Story**
- **Character Trait First**
- **C D A I W P T O**

The structure of *Harry the Dirty Dog* is symmetrical[13], the problem type is "character transformation," and the storytelling strategy is C D A I W P T O (Character Trait, Development, Action, Improved, Worse, Problem, Transformation, Outcome).

Act I: [C]: Introduces character flaw at the very beginning: Harry doesn't like taking baths.

The Rest of Act I: [D]: Development: Shows problematic behavior stemming from that character flaw: Harry steals the scrubbing brush from the tub and buries it in the back yard.

Plot Twist I: [A]: The main character is pulled in the direction of his character flaw: Harry runs away from home.

Act II: [I/W]: Main character first enjoys, then suffers the consequences of his character flaw: Harry has fun playing and in the process gets so dirty that he turns into a black dog with white spots. [P]: A "needs satisfaction" problem arises: despite Harry's best efforts, his family doesn't recognize him.

---

[13] The structure of this story is diagrammed in *How to Write a Children's Picture Book Volume I: Structure*. Eve Heidi Bine-Stock, E & E Publishing, 2004.

Plot Twist II: [T]: The problem is solved by re-alization, decision or change of heart: Harry now wants a bath. He digs up the scrubbing brush and takes it upstairs.

Act III: [O]: Life after character's newfound maturity: Harry begs for a bath and is overjoyed that when he is clean, his family recognizes him. He now sleeps with the scrubbing brush tucked under his pillow.

Come Along, Daisy

- A "Character Transformation" Story
- Character Trait First
- C D A I W P T O

The structure of *Come Along, Daisy* is symmetrical, the problem type is "character transformation," and the storytelling strategy is C D A I W P T O (Character Trait, Development, Action, Improved, Worse, Problem, Transformation, Outcome).

Act I: [C]: Introduces a character flaw at the very beginning: Daisy is too curious, too adventurous.

The Rest of Act I: [D]: Development: Shows problematic behavior stemming from that character flaw: Daisy wanders off and ignores her mother when she calls.

Plot Twist I: [A]: The main character is pulled in the direction of his character flaw: Daisy is distracted by a frog that plops nearby.

Act II: [I/W]: Main character first enjoys, then suffers the consequences of his character flaw: Daisy enjoys playing with the frog. When he leaves, Daisy realizes she is all alone and has frightening experiences. [P]: A "needs satisfaction" problem arises: Daisy is afraid.

Plot Twist II: [T]: The problem is solved by realization, decision or change of heart: Daisy now wishes Mama Duck were with her.

Act III: [O]: Life after character's newfound maturity: Daisy is happy to see her mother again and even though Daisy plays with butterflies, she stays close to Mama Duck.

Where the Wild Things Are

- **A "Character Transformation" Story**
- **Character Trait First**
- **C D A I W P T O**

The structure of *Where the Wild Things Are* is symmetrical[14], the problem type is "character transformation," and the storytelling strategy is C D A I W P T O (Character Trait, Development, Action, Improved, Worse, Problem, Transformation, Outcome).

Act I: [C]: Introduces a character flaw at the very beginning: Max is wild.

The Rest of Act I: [D]: Development: Shows problematic behavior stemming from that character flaw: Max hangs his teddy bear, hammers nails into the wall, chases the dog with a fork and talks back to his mother. He is sent to bed without his supper.

Plot Twist I: [A]: The main character is pulled in the direction of his character flaw: Max imagines a forest growing in his room.

Act II: [I/W]: Main character first enjoys, then suffers the consequences of his character flaw: Max journeys to the land of the Wild Things where he tames them and becomes their king and leads them in a wild rumpus until he tires and sends them to bed

---

[14] The structure of this story is diagrammed in *How to Write a Children's Picture Book Volume I: Structure*. Eve Heidi Bine-Stock, E & E Publishing, 2004.

without their supper. [P]: A "needs satisfaction" problem arises: Max is lonely.

Plot Twist II: [T]: The problem is solved by re-alization, decision or change of heart: Max begins to miss home. He realizes that he wants to be "where someone loved him best of all."

Act III: [O]: Life after character's newfound maturity: Max sails home and finds his supper waiting for him. From this Max knows that, even though he has been wild, his mother still loves him.

Bread and Jam for Frances

- **A "Character Transformation" Story**
- **Character Trait First**
- **C D A I W P T O**

The structure of *Bread and Jam for Frances* is symmetrical, the problem type is "character transformation," and the storytelling strategy is C D A I W P T O (Character Trait, Development, Action, Improved, Worse, Problem, Transformation, Outcome).

Act I: [C]: Introduces a character flaw at the very beginning: Frances won't eat anything but bread and jam.

The Rest of Act I: [D]: Development: Shows problematic behavior stemming from that character flaw: Frances continues to refuse to eat anything but bread and jam.

Plot Twist I: [A]: The main character is pulled in the direction of his character flaw: Frances' mother serves Frances only bread and jam for breakfast.

Act II: [I/W]: Main character first enjoys, then suffers the consequences of his character flaw: Frances eats the lunch of bread and jam that her mother prepared, then eats the after-school snack of bread and jam that her mother prepared. Frances becomes less and less enamored of bread and jam. [P]: A "needs satisfaction" problem arises: at dinner, served only bread and jam again, Frances cries.

Plot Twist II: [T]: The problem is solved by re-alization, decision or change of heart: Frances has finally tired of eating only bread and jam. She wants to eat something else.

Act III: [O]: Life after character's newfound maturity: Frances enjoys eating all kinds of food.

The Story of Ferdinand
- **A "Character Validation" Story**
- **Character Trait First**
- **C D A W P V O**

The structure of *The Story of Ferdinand* is symmetrical, the problem type is "character validation," and the storytelling strategy is C D A W P V O (Character Trait, Development, Action, Worse, Problem, Validation, Outcome).

This "character validation" story is the inverse of the preceding "character transformation" stories.

The "character transformation" stories use Act I to show problematic behavior stemming from the negative character trait while this "character validation" story uses Act I to show laudable behavior stemming from the positive character trait.

The "character transformation" stories use Plot Twist I to pull the character in the direction of his character flaw, while this "character validation" story uses Plot Twist I to pull the character in the direction opposite to his positive character trait.

The "character transformation" stories use Plot Twist II to show the character realizing that he must mend his ways, while this "character validation" story uses Plot Twist II to validate his positive character trait.

Let us look closely at *The Story of Ferdinand* :

Act I: [C]: Introduces the positive character trait at the very beginning: In contrast to other bulls that fight all the time, Ferdinand is a peace-loving bull.

The Rest of Act I: [D]: Development: Shows laudable behavior stemming from that character trait: Ferdinand whiles away the time by smelling the flowers under the cork tree.

Plot Twist I: [A]: Something happens that pulls the main character in the direction opposite to his character trait: Ferdinand sits on a bee and runs around puffing and snorting like he's crazy.

Act II: [W]: Main character suffers the consequences of being pulled away from his natural character trait: Since Ferdinand appears to be so fierce, bullfighters take him to a bullfight. [P]: A "needs satisfaction" problem arises: the bullfighters need Ferdinand to be fierce in the bullfighting arena.

Plot Twist II: [V]: Main character exhibits his original character trait and is validated: Ferdinand enters the bullfighting arena and sits and smells the ladies' flowers.

Act III: [O]: Life after the character trait is validated: The bullfighters take Ferdinand back home and he happily returns to smelling the flowers under the cork tree.

Background First
Storytelling Strategies

Until now, we have examined stories that begin with a problem or character trait. Now we shall turn our attention to stories that begin with the background, that is, with what life is like *before* the problem or character trait appears.

"Needs Satisfaction" Stories – B P A W S O Storytelling Strategy

Examples of Background First stories with problems that are about "needs satisfaction" are *Owen, The Stray Dog, Sylvester and the Magic Pebble, Yoko* and *Caps for Sale*.

These stories tend to use the following storytelling strategy:

Act I shows what life is like before the problem occurs. At Plot Twist I the problem occurs. In Act II, a character responds to the problem but things get progressively worse. At Plot Twist II, the problem is solved, the need met. Act III shows life after the problem is solved.

A "shorthand" for this storytelling strategy might be: B P A W S O (Background, Problem, Action, Worse, Solution, Outcome), which could be pronounced "bee-pawso."

The problem is solved either through the action of the main character, or through other characters on behalf of the main character.

"Character Transformation" Stories – B C A I W P T O and B C A W P T O Storytelling Strategies

Background First "character transformation" stories tend to use the following storytelling strategy:

Act I shows what life is like before the character trait is introduced. At Plot Twist I, the character trait—usually a character flaw—is introduced. In Act II, the character is pulled in the direction of his character trait and the character first enjoys, then suffers the consequences of his character flaw. Things get so bad that his character flaw has created a problem—a "needs satisfaction" problem. At Plot Twist II, the character comes to a realization, makes a decision, or has a change of heart which transforms his character and solves his problem. Act III shows life after his newfound maturity.

A "shorthand" for this storytelling strategy might be: B C A I W P T O (Background, Character Trait, Action, Improved/Worse, Problem, Transformation, Outcome), which could be pronounced with a hard "c" and a long "a" to sound like "bee-kay-wopto."

Of course, if the character just suffers as a result of his character trait (instead of first enjoying and then suffering), the "shorthand" would be BCAWPTO

(Background, Character Trait, Worse, Problem, Transformation, Outcome), and could be pronounced with a hard "c" and sound like "bee-kah-wopto"

Background First stories that deal with "character transformation" are not that common, but they do show up in "hybrid" stories such as *Martha Speaks* and *The Selfish Giant* that combine both "needs satisfaction" and "character transformation."

Let us look at some stories to see how all of this works.

Owen

- **A "Needs Satisfaction" Story**
- **Background First**
- **B P A W S O**

The structure of *Owen* is symmetrical[15], the problem type is "needs satisfaction," and the storytelling strategy is B P A W S O (Background, Problem, Action, Worse, Solution, Outcome).

Act I: [B]: Background—shows what life is like before the problem occurs: Little Owen loves his blanket, Fuzzy, and takes it with him everywhere.

Plot Twist I: [P]: Introduces problem: A meddling neighbor, Mrs. Tweezers, tells Owen's parents that he is too old to carry a blanket around.

Act II: [A + W]: A character responds to the problem but things get progressively worse: Owen's parents try, try, try to take Fuzzy away from Owen but he thwarts their every attempt.

Plot Twist II: [S]: The problem is solved, the need met: Owen's mother comes up with a solution: make little handkerchiefs from Fuzzy.

Act III: [O]: Life after the problem is solved: Owen happily takes a Fuzzy-handkerchief with him wherever he goes and everyone else, including Mrs. Tweezers, is happy with this as well.

---

[15] The structure of this story is diagrammed in *How to Write a Children's Picture Book Volume I: Structure*. Eve Heidi Bine-Stock, E & E Publishing, 2004.

The Stray Dog

- **A "Needs Satisfaction" Story**
- **Background First**
- **B P A W S O**

The structure of *The Stray Dog* is symmetrical, the problem type is "needs satisfaction," and the storytelling strategy is B P A W S O (Background, Problem, Action, Worse, Solution, Outcome).

Act I: [B]: Background—shows what life is like before the problem occurs: A family goes on a picnic and plays with a stray dog that shows up. They name him Willy.

Plot Twist I: [P]: Introduces problem: The family must leave Willy behind when they return home because he might belong to someone who would miss him.

Act II: [A + W]: A character responds to the problem but things get progressively worse: The following week, the whole family tries to go about their lives normally but they all miss Willy. Saturday comes around again and the family goes on another picnic. They see the stray dog again but now he is being chased by a dog catcher!

Plot Twist II: [S]: The problem is solved, the need met: The children tell the dog catcher that the dog is theirs.

Act III: [O]: Life after the problem is solved: The children bathe Willy, introduce him to the neighborhood where he meets interesting dogs, and give him his very own bowl and bed.

Sylvester and the Magic Pebble

- **A "Needs Satisfaction" Story**
- **Background First**
- **B P A W S O**

The structure of *Sylvester and the Magic Pebble* is symmetrical[16], the problem type is "needs satisfaction," and the storytelling strategy is B P A W S O (Background, Problem, Action, Worse, Solution, Outcome).

Act I: [B]: Background—shows what life is like before the problem occurs: Sylvester enjoys collecting pebbles "of unusual shape and color." One day he finds a magic pebble.

Plot Twist I: [P]: Introduces problem: Sylvester accidentally uses the magic pebble to turn into a rock and cannot turn back into himself because he cannot hold the magic pebble to make a wish.

Act II: [A + W]: A character responds to the problem but things get progressively worse: Sylvester's loving parents are heartsick as they search for him unsuccessfully. They finally, reluctantly, give up searching and resign themselves to living without their darling son. Time passes, spring comes again and they force themselves to go on a picnic in an attempt to be happy.

---

[16] The structure of this story is diagrammed in *How to Write a Children's Picture Book Volume I: Structure*. Eve Heidi Bine-Stock, E & E Publishing, 2004.

Plot Twist II: [S]: The problem is solved, the need met: Sylvester's father places the magic pebble on the rock on which their picnic lunch is spread out. The rock is actually Sylvester. Sylvester wishes he were himself again, "and in less than an instant, he was!"

Act III: [O]: Life after the problem is solved: Sylvester and his parents are overjoyed to see each other again. Sylvester's father puts the magic pebble away for safekeeping.

Yoko

- **A "Needs Satisfaction" Story**
- **Background First**
- **B P AW S O**

The structure of *Yoko* is symmetrical, the problem type is "needs satisfaction," and the storytelling strategy is B P A W S O (Background, Problem, Action, Worse, Solution, Outcome).

Act I: [B]: Background—shows what life is like before the problem occurs: Yoko's mother prepares Yoko's favorite food—sushi—for Yoko to take to school for lunch.

Plot Twist I: [P]: Introduces problem: The other kids in Yoko's class make fun of Yoko's sushi.

Act II: [A + W]: A character responds to the problem but things get progressively worse: Yoko's teacher tries to help, but the kids continue to make fun of Yoko's food. Then, at the Midpoint, Yoko's teacher gets an idea: she will have an International Food Day so the kids will taste all different kinds of food. Unfortunately, no one even tries Yoko's sushi and Yoko is very unhappy.

Plot Twist II: [S]: The problem is solved, the need met: Timothy is still hungry so he tries Yoko's sushi—and likes it! He asks Yoko for more sushi tomorrow.

Act III: [O]: Life after the problem is solved: Timothy gives Yoko his own coconut crisp, which

Yoko likes "even better than red bean ice cream!" The next day, Yoko and Timothy happily share their favorite foods—including sushi—at lunch together.

Caps for Sale

- A "Needs Satisfaction" Story
- **Background First**
- **B P A W S O**

The structure of *Caps for Sale* is not symmetrical; it is iterative[17]. Nevertheless, *Caps for Sale* uses the same B P A W S O storytelling strategy as the previous five symmetrical stories. Remember, B P A W S O stands for Background, Problem, Action, Worse, Solution, Outcome. The problem type of *Caps for Sale* is "needs satisfaction."

Act I: [B]: Background—shows what life is like before the problem occurs: The Peddler has an unsuccessful morning selling caps. He then walks to the country and takes a nap under a tree.

Plot Twist I: [P]: Introduces problem: When the Peddler awakes, he discovers that all but one cap is missing.

Act II: [A + W]: A character responds to the problem but things get progressively worse: The Peddler can't find his caps anywhere until he sees monkeys in the tree, wearing his caps. No matter how hard he tries, he can't get the monkeys to give him his caps. They just mimic everything he does.

---

[17] See the Appendix for a definition of the Iterative Paradigm.

Plot Twist II: [S]: The problem is solved, the need met: mimicking the Peddler, the monkeys take off the caps and throw them on the ground.

Act III: [O]: Life after the problem is solved: The Peddler collects the caps, and goes on his way back into town to continue trying to sell them.

Action First
Storytelling Strategies

Some stories begin with a character's interesting behavior and "string us along" for a while before we find out the reason for the behavior. These are Action First stories.

Examples of Action First stories are *Good Night, Gorilla* and *A Chair for My Mother*.

Action First stories are not very common, but it is worthwhile to take a look at them for what they can teach us.

Good Night, Gorilla

- **A "Needs Satisfaction" Story**
- **Action First**

As with many stories, the structure of *Good Night, Gorilla* is symmetrical[18] and the problem type is "needs satisfaction." But *Good Night, Gorilla* is that rare animal, the Action First story.

By beginning the story with Action, and never stating the Problem, we are kept in suspense. We have a mystery. We see the Gorilla and other animals following the Night Watchman and we wonder where they are going. We do not know what their goal is, what need they are trying to satisfy.

Only when the Gorilla and his friends settle in for the night in the Night Watchman's bedroom do we understand their goal. The Gorilla wants to sleep in the Night Watchman's bed—this is the need that he is trying to satisfy.

The first half of the story can be written in "shorthand" by A I S (Action, Improved, Solution).

If the problem is solved half-way through the story, what takes up the second half of the story?

In the Second Half of Act II, the Wife "un-does" the solution by taking the Gorilla back to the zoo. In "shorthand" this is A W (Action, Worse).

---

[18] The structure of this story is diagrammed in *How to Write a Children's Picture Book Volume I: Structure*. Eve Heidi Bine-Stock, E & E Publishing, 2004.

Then from Plot Twist II to the end, the Gorilla follows the Wife back to bed, solving his problem again, this time for good. The "shorthand" for this is A I S O (Action, Improved, Solution, Outcome).

Let us take a look at that again.

A I S—A W—A I S O

Act I to the Midpoint is A I S.

Second Half of Act II is A W.

Plot Twist II to the end is A I S O.

It is easy to see from this that the Gorilla solves his problem *twice*. By omitting statement of the Problem and its Development, the author made room in the story for the Gorilla to solve his problem twice.

And, as we said before, omitting statement of the Problem very effectively creates suspense and a mystery.

Following is a detailed breakdown of the story:

Act I: [P]: Introduces problem at the very beginning: Omitted. [D]: Shows or elaborates the problem: Omitted. [A]: A character sets out to solve the problem: The Gorilla steals the Night Watchman's keys and unlocks the door to his cage and starts to follow the Night Watchman on his rounds of the zoo.

Plot Twist I: [I]: Things get progressively better (for the Gorilla and his animal friends): The Gorilla begins to unlock the cages of his animal friends.

First Half of Act II: [S]: The problem is solved, the need met: The Gorilla and his animal friends follow the Night Watchman into his bedroom and settle down for the night—with the Gorilla in bed with the Night Watchman and his Wife. [Now we understand what the problem was that the Gorilla was trying to solve: he wanted to sleep in bed.]

Midpoint: When the Night Watchman says Goodnight to his Wife, the focus of the story shifts to the Wife.

Second Half of Act II: [A/W]: Things get progressively worse (for the Gorilla and his animal friends): The Wife takes the Gorilla and his animal friends back to their cages in the zoo.

Plot Twist II: [A/I]: Things get progressively better (for the Gorilla and his friend, the Mouse): The Gorilla and Mouse follow the Wife back home and into the bedroom.

Act III: [S]: The problem is solved, the need met: the Gorilla and Mouse are back in bed with the Night Watchman and his Wife—and neither person realizes it. [O]: Life after the problem is solved: The Mouse whispers "Good night" to the Gorilla but he doesn't hear because he is already fast asleep.

A Chair for My Mother

A Chair for My Mother is both an Action First story and a two-problem story. It is discussed in depth in the section on Two-Problem Stories.

Two-Problem Stories

This chapter deals with stories that have two problems to solve rather than one.

We shall see that such a story may combine two problems of the same type—two "needs satisfaction" problems, for example, as in *Corduroy*—or combine different types of problems—a "character validation" problem with a "needs frustration" problem, for example, as in *Fish is Fish*.

We shall also see that two-problem stories employ storytelling strategies that we are familiar with from our study of one-problem stories.

This chapter does not provide an exhaustive look at all possible combinations of problem types and storytelling strategies, but it does show that two-problem stories may be built using the same or similar problem types and storytelling strategies as one-problem stories.

This chapter also shows some of the ways that two problems can be incorporated into stories whose structures follow the Symmetrical Paradigm.

Corduroy

- **A "Needs Satisfaction" Story**
- **Problem First**
- **Two Problems**

The structure of *Corduroy* is symmetrical[19], the problem type is "needs satisfaction," and the storytelling strategy is a variation of P D A W S O (Problem, Development, Action, Worse, Solution, Outcome).

This story has two problems to solve: Corduroy wants someone to take him home [P1], and he is missing a button [P2].

Corduroy fits two problems into one symmetrical story block.

The first problem [P1] is introduced at the very beginning of the story; the second problem [P2] is introduced at the very end of Act I. Plot Twist II solves P1, then, in Act III, P2 is solved, too.

Therefore, the order in which the problems are introduced and the order in which they are solved can be written in "shorthand" like this: P1 P2 S1 S2.

Life after each problem is solved can be indicated by O1 and O2 (O for Outcome).

As we shall see, the storytelling strategy of *Corduroy* as a whole is P1 D P2 A W S1 O1 S2 O2. It is easy to see from this "shorthand" that this is a variation of the P D A W S O strategy.

---

[19] The structure of this story is diagrammed in *How to Write a Children's Picture Book Volume I: Structure.* Eve Heidi Bine-Stock, E & E Publishing, 2004.

Let us see how this breaks down:

Act I: [P1]: Introduces problem at the very beginning: Corduroy wants someone to take him home.

The Rest of Act I: [D]: Development: Shows or elaborates the problem: The store is always filled with shoppers but no one wants Corduroy. The little girl's mother doesn't want him because she's spent too much money already and he doesn't look new because he's lost a button. ([P2]: This missing button is a secondary problem which introduces a subplot.)

Plot Twist I: [A]: A character sets out to solve the problem: Corduroy sets out to find his missing button.

Act II: [W]: Things get progressively worse: Corduroy searches through the store and gets into all kinds of mischief.

Plot Twist II: [S1]: The main problem is solved, the need met: The little girl returns to the store to take Corduroy home.

Act III: [O1]: Life after the main problem is solved: Corduroy, now at home in the little girl's room, is happy to see his very own bed. [S2]: The little girl sews a new button on Corduroy's overalls. [O2]: Life after the secondary problem is solved: Corduroy and the little girl hug each other; they've always wanted a friend.

Lilly's Purple Plastic Purse
- **A "Needs Satisfaction" Story**
- **Background First**
- **Two Problems**

Lilly's Purple Plastic Purse is a symmetrical "needs satisfaction" story that has two problems: Lilly can't control her desire to show everyone her new purse [P1], and she feels guilty and ashamed about her behavior toward her teacher [P2]. Lilly's idea of the solution to her first problem actually contributes to her second problem.

Lilly's Purple Plastic Purse fits two problems into one symmetrical story block.

The first problem is introduced at Plot Twist I; the second problem is introduced at the Midpoint. At Plot Twist II, Lilly's apology solves both problems satisfactorily.

As we shall see, *Lilly's Purple Plastic Purse* employs two overlapping storytelling strategies:

B P A W S O and B P A W I S O.

Note that the second strategy, B P A **W I** S O, is a variation of the more usual B P A **W** S O. In *Lilly's Purple Plastic Purse*, after the second problem arises, things go from **Worse** to **Improved** (rather than just the more usual **Worse** that we see in "needs satisfaction" stories) once Lilly's parents become involved and they help her prepare to apologize.

Let us see how the story breaks down:

Act I: [B1]: Background—shows what life is like before the problem occurs: Lilly loves school, is exuberant, loves her teacher and craves his attention. She wants to be a teacher when she grows up.

Plot Twist I: [P1]: Introduces first problem: Lilly brings her new purse to school and interrupts class to show it to everyone.

First Half of Act II: [A1]: A character responds to the problem: Lilly's teacher takes Lilly's purse away. [W1]: Things get progressively worse: Lilly gets more and more upset and angry. She draws a hateful picture and writes a hateful note.

Midpoint: [S1—Lilly's idea of a solution]: Lilly leaves the hateful note and drawing in her teacher's book bag. [O1]: Life after the problem is "solved": Lilly discovers that her teacher left a nice note and treats in her purse when he returned it to her. [This [O1] also serves as the Background [B2] to the following problem]: [P2]: Lilly now feels guilty and ashamed.

Second Half of Act II: [A2]: A character sets out to solve the problem: Lilly runs home to tell her parents what happened. [W2]: Things get progressively worse: Lilly is miserable; she punishes herself. [I2]: Things get progressively better: Lilly's parents help her prepare to apologize by baking treats and preparing a new letter and drawing of apology.

Plot Twist II: [S1+S2]: The first and second problems are solved, the needs met: Lilly apologizes to her teacher.

Act III: [O1+O2]: Life after the problems are solved: At an appropriate time, Lilly shows her purse to her class and the rest of the day doesn't disturb the others about it. Lilly is happy again and again wants to be a teacher when she grows up.

The Selfish Giant

- **Hybrid "Character Transformation" and "Needs Satisfaction" Story**
- **Background First**
- **Two Problems**

The Selfish Giant is a combination of a "character transformation" story and a "needs satisfaction" story. There are two problems here. As soon as one problem is solved, the second problem appears.

The first problem is that the Giant is selfish. This is what the "character transformation" aspect of the story is about. But as soon as the Giant mends his ways, he has a new problem: he misses the little boy who kissed him. This is what the "needs satisfaction" aspect of the story is about.

The Selfish Giant fits two problems into one symmetrical story block.

The Selfish Giant brings up the first problem at Plot Twist I and solves it at the Mid-Spot[20], then brings up the second problem in the Second Half of Act II, and solves it at Plot Twist II. Note that *The Selfish Giant* doesn't bring up the second problem until the first problem is solved.

As we shall see, *The Selfish Giant* employs two overlapping storytelling strategies: B C A W P T O and B P A W S O.

Let us see how all of this breaks down:

---

[20] For a definition of Mid-Spot, see the Appendix.

Act I: [B]: Background—shows what life is like before the character flaw is introduced: While the Giant is away, the children play in his garden. [C]: The character trait is introduced: The Giant is a low character. He has been visiting his friend the Cornish ogre, which reflects badly on his own character since we are judged by the company we keep.

Plot Twist I: [A]: The main character is pulled in the direction of his character flaw: The Giant returns and selfishly bans the children from his garden.

First Half of Act II: [W]: Main character suffers the consequences of his character flaw: Winter stays in the garden. As long as the children are absent from the garden, spring does not return. [P]: A "needs satisfaction" problem arises: The Giant misses spring.

Mid-Spot: [T]: The first problem is solved by realization, decision or change of heart: The children creep back into the garden and spring returns to most of it, but one corner of the garden remains winter because a little boy is too small to climb up on the tree there. The boy cries and the Giant's heart melts: he is now sorry for having been so selfish—the first problem is solved.

Second Half of Act II: [O]: Life after the character's newfound maturity: The Giant sets the little boy on the tree and the little boy kisses the Giant. The Giant lets all the children come to his garden whenever they want and it is now eternally spring there. [This [O] also serves as the Background [B2] to the following problem]: [P2]: The second problem arises when the Giant can't find the little boy again. [A2]: A character sets out to solve the problem: The Giant asks the other children about him but they don't know who he is. [W2]: Things get progressively worse: The Giant misses the little boy and longs to see him again. Years pass.

Plot Twist II: [S2]: The second problem is solved, the need met: The little boy returns.

Act III: [O2]: Life after the second problem is solved: We learn that the little boy is The Savior; he has come to take the now elderly Giant to Paradise. The children come to the garden later that day and find the Giant dead under a tree, covered with white blossoms.

Martha Speaks

- **Hybrid "Character Transformation" and "Needs Satisfaction" Story**
- **Background First**
- **Two Problems**

Martha Speaks is a combination of a "character transformation" story and a "needs satisfaction" story. Story Block I focuses on character transformation while Story Block II focuses on satisfying a need. *Martha Speaks* thus has two problems to solve: talking too much and foiling a burglar.

Unlike *The Selfish Giant* which fits two problems into one symmetrical story block, *Martha Speaks* combines two symmetrical story blocks that overlap each other: Act III of Story Block I also serves as Act I of Story Block II. (Rather than being an exception to the Symmetrical Paradigm, *Martha Speaks* is really a more sophisticated example of it.)

As we shall see, *Martha Speaks* employs two overlapping storytelling strategies: B A C I W P T O and B P A W S O.

It is interesting to note that the storytelling strategy of the first story block is B **A C** I W P T O instead of the more usual B **C A** I W P T O. That is, in *Martha Speaks*, the action *precedes* the character trait. The action is the letters going to Martha's brain; the character trait is her ability to speak.

Let us see how all of this works:

Story Block I:

Act I: [B]: Background—shows what life is like before the character trait is introduced: Helen doesn't want to eat her soup so she gives it to Martha dog to eat. [A]: The main character is pulled in the direction of his character trait: The letters go to Martha's brain instead of her stomach.

Plot Twist I: [C]: The character trait is introduced: Martha speaks. She had a lot to say and now has the opportunity to say it.

Act II: [I/W]: Main character first enjoys, then suffers the consequences of his character trait: Martha first amazes and delights people with her ability to speak, and then annoys and embarrasses them because she says whatever she thinks. [P]: A "needs satisfaction" problem arises: Martha can't control what she says.

Plot Twist II: [T]: The problem is solved by realization, decision or change of heart: The family tells her to "shut up" and she's crushed.

Act III: [O]: Life after character's newfound maturity: Martha won't speak anymore and she stops eating alphabet soup.

Story Block II:

Act I: [B]: Background—shows what life is like before the problem occurs: Martha doesn't speak.

Plot Twist I: [P]: Introduces problem: A burglar breaks into the house.

Act II: [A]: A character sets out to solve the problem: Martha dials 911. [W]: Things get progressively worse: Martha can't tell the police what's wrong. She barks and growls at the burglar but he's not scared away. He grabs a pot and Martha thinks he's going to hit her with it.

Plot Twist II: [S]: The problem is solved, the need met: The burglar places the pot on the floor to feed Martha and keep her occupied. The pot contains alphabet soup!

Act III: [O]: Life after the problem is solved: Martha calls the police; the burglar is caught. Martha resumes eating alphabet soup every day and now learns "what to say and when to say it."

At the end of Story Block I of *Martha Speaks*, the solution to the first problem (she talks too much) is actually an over-correction (she stops speaking altogether) and is just a temporary solution.

It isn't till the very end of the story, in Act III of Story Block II, that the problem is resolved completely and satisfactorily (she learns when to speak and what to say).

Act III of Story Block II therefore serves to tie up the loose ends of *both* Story Block I and Story Block II.

Tikki Tikki Tembo

- **"Needs Satisfaction" Story**
- **Background First**
- **Two Problems**

Tikki Tikki Tembo has one problem to solve—twice. First one brother falls into a well and must be saved, then the other brother falls into the same well and must be similarly saved. The problem type is therefore "needs satisfaction."

Tikki Tikki Tembo combines two symmetrical story blocks by devoting one symmetrical story block to each brother. Unlike *Martha Speaks*, the story blocks do not overlap; one story block follows the other without any overlap.

Each story block employs the B P A W S O storytelling strategy (Background, Problem, Action, Worse, Solution, Outcome).

Story Block I:

Act I: [B1]: Background—shows what life is like before the problem occurs: We learn the ancient Chinese custom for naming first and second sons. Second sons were given very short names, while first, honored sons were given great long names.

Plot Twist I: [P1]: Introduces problem: The second son, Chang, falls into the well.

Act II: [A1]: A character sets out to solve the problem: The first son, Tikki Tikki Tembo-no sa rembo-chari bari ruchi-pip peri pembo, runs to tell his mother. [W1]: Things get progressively worse: His mother is washing clothes at the river and cannot hear him over the roar of the water.

Plot Twist II: [S1]: The problem is solved, the need met: The old man with the ladder hurries to save the second son, Chang.

Act III: [O1]: Life after the problem is solved: With the water pushed out of him, and the air pushed into him, Chang is soon as good as ever.

Story Block II:

Act I: [B2]: Background—shows what life is like before the problem occurs: The boys celebrate the Festival of the Eighth Moon.

Plot Twist I: [P2]: Introduces problem: The first son, Tikki Tikki Tembo-no sa rembo-chari bari ruchi-pip peri pembo, falls into the well.

Act II: [A2]: A character sets out to solve the problem: The second son, Chang, runs to tell his mother. [W2]: Things get progressively worse: First, his mother is washing clothes at the river and cannot hear him over the roar of the water. Then Chang takes so long, and stumbles so much over his brother's name, that his mother fails to understand him, becomes exasperated, and chastises him. Finally, in spite of the long name he must pronounce, Chang makes himself understood to his mother.

Plot Twist II: [S2]: The problem is solved, the need met: The old man with the ladder hurries to save the first son, Tikki Tikki Tembo-no sa rembo-chari bari ruchi-pip peri pembo.

Act III: [O2]: Life after the problem is solved: Even after the water is pushed out of him, and the air pushed into him, "the moon rose many times before" Tikki Tikki Tembo-no sa rembo-chari bari ruchi-pip peri pembo "was quite the same again." Due to the problem caused by the first son's long name, the Chinese changed their custom for giving names and now "thought it wise to give all their children little, short names instead of great long names."

Fish is Fish

- **Hybrid "Character Validation" and "Needs Frustration" Story**
- **Background First**
- **Two Problems**

Fish is Fish is a combination of a "character validation" story and a "needs frustration" story. The tadpole who turns into a frog is validated for being a frog, while the fish who wants to be like the frog is frustrated in his desire.

The "character validation" story of the frog spans the entire symmetrical structure of *Fish is Fish* while the "needs frustration" story of the fish begins at the Midpoint and continues to the end.

As we shall see, *Fish is Fish* employs two over-lapping storytelling strategies: B C D A I P V O and B P D A W F O. While we have not encountered these precise strategies before, it is easy to see that they are variations of ones we have.

The B C D A I P V O storytelling strategy of the frog's "character validation" story shares much in common with the C D A W P V O storytelling strategy employed in *The Story of Ferdinand*, another "character validation" story. The differences are that the frog's story provides background [B] first, and things progressively improve for the frog [I], rather than worsen [W].

The B P D A W F O storytelling strategy of the fish's "needs frustration" story shares elements with the P D A I F O storytelling strategy of *The Wolf's Chicken Stew*, another "needs frustration" story. The differences are that the fish's story provides background [B] first, and things worsen for the fish [W], rather than improve [I].

Both stories fit within one symmetrical structure.

Let us see how the stories of the frog and the fish break down:

Frog's Story:

Act I: [B]: Background—shows what life is like before the character trait is introduced: A minnow and a tadpole live in a pond and are inseparable friends.

Pinch I[21]: [C]: The character trait is introduced: The tadpole grows two little legs. Now he knows his true character: he is a frog.

The Rest of Act I: [D]: Development: The tadpole continues to grow frog-like characteristics until he is a real frog.

Plot Twist I: [A]: Something happens that pulls the main character in the direction of his character trait: The frog climbs out of the water and onto the grassy bank.

Act II: [I]: Main character enjoys the consequences of his character trait: The frog is absent from the pond while he explores the world, then returns to the pond and regales the fish with stories about all the

---

[21] See the Appendix for definitions of *Pinch I* and *Pinch II*.

fantastic creatures he has seen on land. [P]: A "needs satisfaction" problem arises: The fish wants to be like the frog and see the fantastic creatures for himself, so...

Plot Twist II: [P]: ...the fish jumps out of the water onto the bank.

Pinch II: [V]: Main character exhibits his original character trait and is validated: The frog, who now lives on land, sees his friend gasping for air and pushes him back into the water.

Act III: [O]: Life after the character trait is validated: Because the frog *is* a frog and can live on land, he was able to save his friend the fish. The fish further validates the frog's character trait by admitting that the frog was right: frogs are frogs and "fish is fish."

Fish's Story

Midpoint: [B]: Background—shows what life is like before the problem occurs: The fish listens while the frog regales him with stories of the fantastic creatures that live on land.

Second Half of Act II: [P]: Introduces problem: The fish wants to be like the frog and see the fantastic creatures for himself. [D]: Development: Shows or elaborates the problem: As the days go by, the fish dreams about the fantastic creatures that live on land.

Plot Twist II: [A]: A character sets out to solve the problem: The fish jumps out of the water onto the bank.

Act III: [W]: Things get worse: The fish gasps for air and is unable to breathe or to move.

Pinch II [F]: The problem is not solved, the need is *not* met: The fish cannot live on land. He will never be like his friend the frog; he will never see those fantastic creatures. Luckily for him, his friend the frog sees him gasping for air and pushes him back into the water.

The Rest of Act III: [O]: Life after the problem is not solved, the need is *not* met: The fish, back in the pond, recovers and smiles at his friend the frog who now watches him from a lily leaf. The fish admits that the frog was right: frogs are frogs and fish is fish. The fish is now satisfied with his own world.

A Chair for My Mother

- **A "Needs Satisfaction" Story**
- **Action First**
- **Two Problems**

Hold on to your hats! *A Chair for My Mother* is both an Action First story and a two-problem story. It begins with the Action of the girl and her mother saving coins.

As with *Good Night, Gorilla*, by beginning the story with Action, instead of stating the Problem, we are kept in suspense. We have a mystery: what are the girl and her mother saving their coins for?

While *Good Night, Gorilla* never does state the Problem, *A Chair for My Mother* does.

In fact, there are two Problems: saving enough money to fill the jar, and finding a "wonderful, beautiful, fat, soft armchair...covered in velvet with roses all over it."

The statement of these Problems is made *after* we see the Action of saving coins. This means that the reason for the Action is given *after* we see the Action. And to top it off, the Background to the Problems is introduced even later, as a flashback. The Background is the story of the fire and the destruction of all of their belongings, including all of their chairs.

The story about the coins-and-jar, and the story about the chair, are each given the same number of pages in the book.

The storytelling strategy of the coins-and-jar story is A P B A I S O. The storytelling strategy of the chair story is P B A W S O. Remember, A P B A I S O stands for Action, Problem, Background, Action, Improved, Solution, Outcome. P B A W S O stands for Problem, Background, Action, Worse, Solution, Outcome.

The first half of *A Chair for My Mother* combines the A P B of the coins-and-jar story with the P B of the chair story.

The first Problem (filling the jar with coins) must be solved before the second Problem (finding the chair) can be.

In the second half of *A Chair for My Mother*, the Action of saving coins is picked up again (after the interlude of the Background) and things get progressively better regarding filling the jar with coins until at last the jar is full. The girl puts the coins in paper wrappers and then she and her mother go to the bank to exchange the coins for bills. The storytelling strategy of this portion of the coins-and-jar story is Action, Improved, Solution, Outcome: A I S O.

After the Problem of the coins is solved, the Problem of finding the right chair must be solved. The girl, her mother, and grandmother take the bus downtown and shop through four furniture stores. They try out so many chairs that they feel like Goldilocks in the story of the Three Bears, until, finally, they find the chair they have been dreaming of. Then we hear what life is like after they find the chair. The storytelling strategy of this portion of the chair story is Action, Worse, Solution, Outcome: A W S O.

By combining the A P B A I S O of the coins-and-jar story with the P B A W S O of the chair story, we can describe both halves of *A Chair for My Mother* with the following "shorthand":

A1 P1 P2 B1+2—A1 I1 S1 O1—A2 W2 S2 O2

If this looks too much like algebra, just remember that it is a combination of A P B A I S O and P B A W S O, and that in the first half of *A Chair for My Mother*, the Action comes first, then the Problem, then the Background. The second half of *A Chair for My Mother* continues with the more conventional storytelling strategies of A I S O and A W S O.

Let us take a closer look at the Background portion of the story. When we look inside it, we see that the storytelling strategy of the Background is the more conventional B P A I S O, with the Background to the Problem coming first and then the Problem:

[B]: Background—shows what life is like before the problem occurs: The girl and her mother are coming home from buying new shoes and admiring tulips along the way.

[P]: Introduces the problem: They see fire engines and smoke outside their house and flames coming from the roof. Their house is on fire. It is destroyed and all of their belongings are ruined.

[A]: A character responds to the problem: When they move into a new apartment, the neighbors bring them food and furniture...

[I]: Things get progressively better: ...and a rug, curtains, pots and pans, silverware, dishes and a stuffed bear.

[S]: The problem is solved; the need met: The girl and her mother and grandmother have the basics that they need.

[O]: Life after the problem is solved: Grandma makes a speech, thanking everyone for their help in starting over.

The above is the Background to both the coins-and-jar story and the chair story. The Background is a small, complete story within the bigger stories and as we have seen, it employs the more conventional storytelling strategy of B P A I S O.

Afterword: The Emotional Nature of Writing

Although we have discussed many techniques and "rules" of writing, the experience of writing is, at its core, a very emotional one.

We write first of all because we feel something that we want others to feel. We write because we want to recreate through words on paper a sequence of events—a story—that will stir in the reader a specific emotional experience.

Children's picture storybooks seem simple, but reading, and writing, them is emotionally complex.

As we write, we must constantly compare how we feel with the goal feeling we are trying to achieve. And we tweak and edit until what we feel coincides with the goal feeling.

As we write, we are constantly aware of the difference between what the characters feel in the midst of their situation, and what the reader feels as observer. We feel *both* what the character feels and what the outsider looking in—the "objective" reader—feels. We have mixed feelings.

Every scene, Beat, Link, sentence, word, comma and period is an emotional experience. If you do it right, the act of writing is emotionally draining—and exhilarating!

Appendix—Definitions

To see how the terms defined here are applied to popular picture storybooks, see Volume I of this series, *How to Write a Children's Picture Book.* Eve Heidi Bine-Stock, E & E Publishing, 2004.

Iterative Paradigm

The Iterative Paradigm is a description of the structure of some picture storybooks in which the page pattern of the second half of the story simply repeats the pattern of the first half. For example, the page pattern might be:

Act I	1st Half Act II	Mid-Point	2nd Half Act II	Act III
3	6	1	3	6

or

Act I	1st Half Act II	Mid-Point	2nd Half Act II	Act III
6	3	1	6	3

Mike Mulligan and His Steam Shovel is an example of a picture storybook that follows the Iterative Paradigm.

A detailed definition of the Iterative Paradigm, and how it applies to selected picture storybooks, appears in Volume I of this series, *How to Write a Children's Picture Book*. Eve Heidi Bine-Stock, E & E Publishing, 2004.

Mid-Point & Mid-Spot

The Mid-Point is an incident that occurs right in the middle of Act II; it is a pivotal incident that divides Act II into the First Half of Act II and the Second Half of Act II.

Whereas the Mid-Point is a single incident that takes up only one or two pages, the Mid-Spot is an *interlude* in the middle of the story that takes up four to five pages.

A more detailed definition of Mid-Point and Mid-Spot, together with examples in popular picture storybooks, appears in Volume I of this series, *How to Write a Children's Picture Book*. Eve Heidi Bine-Stock, E & E Publishing, 2004.

Pinches I & II

A Pinch is something that happens—an action or event—that keeps the story moving on track. The Pinch propels the story *forward*. It is a moment of punctuation in the story line. If a story has a Pinch at all, it comes in pairs—Pinch I in Act I and Pinch II in Act III.

A more detailed definition of Pinches I and II, together with examples of Pinches in popular picture storybooks, appears in Volume I of this series, *How to Write a Children's Picture Book*. Eve Heidi Bine-Stock, E & E Publishing, 2004.

Plot Twists I & II

Plot Twist I is an action or event that serves as punctuation between Act I and Act II. It spins the story off in a new direction; *it is a turning point.*

Plot Twist II is a similar punctuation that signifies the end of Act II and the start of Act III. It is an action or event that spins the story off in a new direction. *It is the turning point that leads to the resolution.*

A more detailed definition of Plot Twist I and II, together with examples of Plot Twists in popular picture storybooks, appears in Volume I of this series, *How to Write a Children's Picture Book*. Eve Heidi Bine-Stock, E & E Publishing, 2004.

Symmetrical Paradigm

The Symmetrical Paradigm is a description of the structure of many picture storybooks in which the two halves of the story are mirror images of each other. An example of the page pattern of a Symmetrical story might be:

Act I	1st Half Act II	Mid-Point	2nd Half Act II	Act III
3	6	1	6	3

Examples of picture storybooks that follow the Symmetrical Paradigm are *Leo the Late Bloomer*, *Harry the Dirty Dog* and *Corduroy*.

A detailed definition of the Symmetrical Paradigm, and how it applies to many picture storybooks, appears in Volume I of this series, *How to Write a Children's Picture Book*. Eve Heidi Bine-Stock, E & E Publishing, 2004.

Bibliography

Bread and Jam for Frances. Russell Hoban. Illustrated by Lillian Hoban. HarperCollins, 1993.

Caps for Sale: A Tale of a Peddler, Some Monkeys and Their Monkey Business. Esphyr Slobodkina. Harper & Row, 1947.

A Chair for My Mother. Vera B. Williams. Greenwillow, 1982.

Come Along, Daisy. Jane Simmons. Little, Brown 1998.

"Cookies" from ***Frog and Toad Together***. Arnold Lobel. Harper & Row, 1972.

Corduroy. Don Freeman. Viking Press, 1968.

Curious George. H.A. Rey. Houghton Mifflin, 1941.

"Dragons and Giants" from ***Frog and Toad Together***. Arnold Lobel. Harper & Row, 1972.

Fish is Fish. Leo Lionni. Pantheon, 1970.

"The Garden" from ***Frog and Toad are Friends***. Arnold Lobel. Harper & Row, 1970.

Good Night, Gorilla. Peggy Rathmann. Putnam, 1994.

Harold and the Purple Crayon. Crockett Johnson. Harper & Row, 1955.

Harry the Dirty Dog. Gene Zion. Illustrated by Margaret Bloy Graham. Harper, 1956.

How to Write a Children's Picture Book Volume I: Structure: Learning from The Very Hungry Caterpillar, Chicka Chicka Boom Boom, Corduroy, Where the Wild Things Are, The Carrot Seed, Good Night, Gorilla, Sylvester and the Magic Pebble, and Other Favorite Stories. Eve Heidi Bine-Stock, E & E Publishing, 2004.

If You Give a Mouse a Cookie. Laura Joffee Numeroff. Illustrated by Felicia Bond. Harper & Row, 1985.

Leo the Late Bloomer. Robert Kraus. Illustrated by Jose Aruego. Windmill Books, 1971.

"The Letter" from ***Frog and Toad are Friends***. Arnold Lobel. Harper & Row, 1970.

Lilly's Purple Plastic Purse. Kevin Henkes. Greenwillow, 1996.

"The List" from ***Frog and Toad Together***. Arnold Lobel. Harper & Row, 1972.

"A Lost Button" from *Frog and Toad are Friends*. Arnold Lobel. Harper & Row, 1970.

Lyle, Lyle, Crocodile. Bernard Waber. Houghton Mifflin, 1965.

Madeline. Ludwig Bemelmans. Simon & Schuster, 1939.

Make Way for Ducklings. Robert McCloskey. Viking Press, 1941.

Martha Speaks. Susan Meddaugh. Houghton Mifflin, 1992.

Mike Mulligan and His Steam Shovel. Virginia Lee Burton. Houghton Mifflin, 1939.

Millions of Cats. Wanda Gág. Coward-McCann, 1928.

Miss Nelson is Missing! Harry Allard. Illustrated by James Marshall. Houghton Mifflin, 1977.

Owen. Kevin Henkes. Greenwillow, 1993.

Rhetorical Grammar: Grammatical Choices, Rhetorical Effects. Third Edition. Martha Kolln. Allyn & Bacon, 1998.

Scene & Structure. Jack M. Bickham. Writer's Digest Books, 1993.

The Selfish Giant. Oscar Wilde. Illustrated by Lizbeth Zwerger. Picture Book Studio USA, 1984.

"Spring" from *Frog and Toad are Friends*. Arnold Lobel. Harper & Row, 1970.

Stone Soup. Marcia Brown. Scribner. 1947.

"The Story" from *Frog and Toad are Friends*. Arnold Lobel. Harper & Row, 1970.

The Story of Ferdinand. Monro Leaf. Viking Press, 1936.

Story: Substance, Structure, Style and the Principles of Screenwriting. Robert McKee. HarperCollins, 1997.

The Stray Dog. Marc Simont. HarperCollins, 2001.

Strega Nona. Tomie De Paola. Prentice-Hall, 1975.

"The Surprise" from *Frog and Toad All Year*. Arnold Lobel. Harper & Row, 1976.

Sylvester and the Magic Pebble. William Steig. Windmill Books, 1969.

Tikki Tikki Tembo. Arlene Mosel. Illustrated by Blair Lent. Holt, Rinehart & Winston, 1968.

Where the Wild Things Are. Maurice Sendak. Harper & Row, 1963.

The Wolf's Chicken Stew. Keiko Kasza. G.P. Putnam's Sons, 1987.

Yoko. Rosemary Wells. Hyperion Books for Children, 1998.

Index

About the Author

Eve Heidi Bine-Stock is the author of Volumes I, II and III of this series, *How to Write a Children's Picture Book*, and has written pseudonymously numerous books for children. Ms. Bine-Stock is also the Publisher of **E & E Publishing** which publishes children's picture books and non-fiction books for adults.

LaVergne, TN USA
12 January 2010
169709LV00004B/174/A